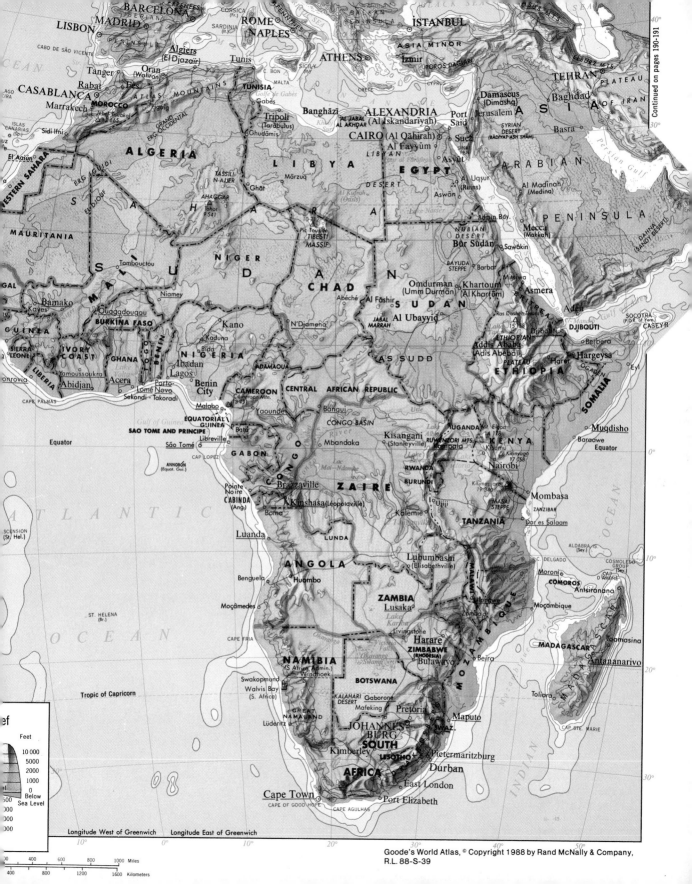

Enchantment of the World

ETHIOPIA

By Dennis Brindell Fradin

Consultant for Ethiopia: James C. McCann, Ph.D., African Studies Center, Boston University, Boston, Massachusetts

Consultant for Reading: Robert L. Hillerich, Ph.D., Bowling Green State University, Bowling Green, Ohio

CHILDRENS PRESS ®

CHICAGO

People from Debre Birhan, just north of Addis Ababa

Library of Congress Cataloging-in-Publication Data

Fradin, Dennis B.
   Ethiopia / by Dennis Brindell Fradin.
      p.   cm. — (Enchantment of the world)
   Includes index.
   Summary: Discusses the geography, history,
government, people, and culture of this triangular east
African country.
   ISBN 0-516-02706-9
   1.   Ethiopia—Juvenile
literature.   [1. Ethiopia.]   I. Title.   II. Series.
DT373.F67   1988   88-10882
963—dc19   CIP
                                                                      AC

Childrens Press®, Chicago
Copyright ©1988 by Regensteiner Publishing Enterprises, Inc.
All rights reserved. Published simultaneously in Canada.
Printed in the United States of America.
1 2 3 4 5 6 7 8 9 10 R 97 96 95 94 93 92 91 90 89 88

Picture Acknowledgments
© **Photri, Inc.:** 4, 6, 8, 14 (right), 32, 34, 61, 64 (2 photos), 65 (bottom, left & right), 68, 69 (bottom), 72 (top left), 81 (right), 88 (left), 93, 99, 100 (bottom left & right), 112

© **Shostal Associates:** cover inset, 5, 10, 12, 13, 15 (left), 18 (left), 22 (2 photos), 60, 62, 65 (top), 67 (2 photos), 69 (top), 72 (top right), 74 (top), 76 (bottom right), 86 (left), 97 (left), 98 (right), 109
Valan Photos: © Christine Osborne: 6 (inset), 17 (2 photos), 66 (top, left & right), 70 (right), 81 (left), 86 (right), 91 (left); © Kennon Cooke: 18 (right); © B. Lyon: 18 (top), 19 (top left); © Aubrey Long: 19 (top, middle & right); © Stephen J. Krasemann: 19 (bottom, left & right)
© **Bob & Ira Spring:** 14 (left), 76 (top), 92, 105
© **Victor Englebert:** 15 (right), 16 (2 photos), 23 (2 photos), 26 (2 photos), 27 (2 photos), 57, 58, 66 (bottom), 70 (left, top & bottom), 71 (2 photos), 72 (bottom), 74 (bottom), 76 (bottom left), 78 (2 photos), 79 (2 photos), 80 (2 photos), 82 (4 photos), 85 (2 photos), 87 (2 photos), 88 (right), 89, 91 (right), 96, 98 (left), 100 (top left & top right)
Root Resources: © Anthony Mercieca: 18 (middle)
Historical Pictures Service, Chicago: 36 (2 photos), 38, 40, 45
AP/Wide World Photos, Inc.: 43, 46 (2 photos), 51, 53 (2 photos)
UN Photo: © John Isaac: 55
The Image Bank: © Miguel, 94
H. Armstrong Roberts: © Zefa H. Honkanen: cover; © John Moss: 97 (right)
Len W. Meents: Maps on pages 13, 58, 63, 69, 74
Courtesy Flag Research Center, Winchester, Massachusetts 01890: Flag on back cover
Cover: The city of Asmara, Ethiopia
Cover inset: Native dwellings near
                        Debre Libanos

A basket weaver

TABLE OF CONTENTS

Right: A field full of flowers after the September rains
Below: The fertile land and mountains near Jima

Chapter 1

THE LAND OF
THE LION OF JUDAH

Ethiopia is a mountainous country in northeastern Africa. Ethiopia has a great deal of fertile land with rolling green meadows that are covered with beautiful flowers after the September rains. It also has vast regions so rugged that they resemble the surface of the moon. Steep mountains and deep canyons make it difficult to travel within Ethiopia. And the country's desert regions have been known to reach the unearthly temperature of 120 degrees Fahrenheit (48.9 degrees Celsius).

Ethiopia's history is as varied as its terrain. For many centuries the country was ruled by powerful emperors. Ethiopia's provinces were required to send the emperor tributes consisting of gold, honey, livestock, frankincense, and slaves. A number of emperors were respected for their scholarship, fairness, and for leading Ethiopia to victory in battle. Due partly to the emperors' immense power, Ethiopia was never colonized by a European nation. Ethiopia's more than two thousand years of independence make it Africa's oldest independent country.

Awash River gorge in Awash National Park

Several military events of global importance have occurred in
Ethiopia. In 1896 the Ethiopian army crushed Italian forces in the
Battle of Adowa in northern Ethiopia. This marked an important
victory over a European army by African forces and preserved
Ethiopia's independence. Nearly forty years later, in 1935, Italian
soldiers marched into Ethiopia and defeated the Ethiopian troops
with a modern air force and poison gas. Italy's invasion of
Ethiopia was one of the major events that led to World War II.

Despite its often violent history, Ethiopia has made some vital
contributions to world culture. An interesting form of poetry
called "wax and gold" originated in Ethiopia, along with the
Semitic language family. Several important events in the history
of three religions—Judaism, Christianity, and Islam—also
occurred here.

A famous biblical story concerns Solomon, king of Israel, and

Sheba, queen of Ethiopia. While visiting Solomon, Sheba became pregnant by him. Their son—Menilek I—became Ethiopia's first emperor. Most later Ethiopian emperors claimed to be descendants of Solomon and Sheba, and Ethiopia has been called the Solomonic Empire and its ruler, the Lion of Judah. The country's most recent emperor, Haile Sellassie I, claimed to be 225th in the long line of rulers descended from the biblical pair, although of course that cannot be proved.

According to tradition, Christianity was introduced into Ethiopia in about A.D. 300 by two Christian youths who were shipwrecked along the Red Sea and converted the king. Although this is another story that cannot be proved, it is a fact that Christianity came to Ethiopia at about that time. Because Ethiopia is isolated by rough terrain from other Christian nations, it developed its own form of Ethiopian Orthodox Christianity. Ethiopian Christianity is similar to Russian and Greek Orthodox religions. Because Judaism was important in Ethiopia at that time, some practices of Ethiopian Christianity—such as diet restrictions and music—resemble Jewish traditions.

Islam was brought to Ethiopia in the mid-600s by followers of Muhammad, the religion's founder. When some of his disciples were persecuted in what is now Saudi Arabia, Muhammad told them to go to Ethiopia, "a land of justice, where God will bring you rest from your afflictions." These were the first of many millions of Islamic people to bring their faith to Ethiopia. Many Ethiopians have come to accept Islam as their religion.

A minority of the population, mostly in the south and west, follow their traditional religions with their own god and customs of worship. The country also has a few thousand people known as *Falashas*, who practice an Ethiopian version of Judaism.

Farmers near Asmara

Some residents of Addis Ababa and the other larger cities live the same as people in more advanced countries. However, most Ethiopians are subsistence farmers—people who even in the best of times produce barely enough food to feed their families. During the worst of times, such as when there is a drought, many subsistence farmers may die of hunger and disease.

Ethiopia's lack of progress in combating hunger, disease, and poverty over the years has left it one of the world's least developed nations. Ethiopia has had the tragic distinction of being one of the world's ten poorest countries; of having one of the lowest life expectancies (about forty-three years) of any nation on earth; and of having one of the lowest literacy rates. In 1974 less than 5 percent of the people could read and write, but a program of teaching has raised the literacy rate to almost 30 percent.

Large-scale discontent over the problems of poverty and the needs of modernization led Ethiopians to revolt against their traditional form of government in 1974. That year Emperor Haile Sellassie was deposed, ending several thousand years of rule by the country's emperors. The new military rulers set up a Socialist state in Ethiopia. This revolution was accomplished with a terrible amount of bloodshed, but Ethiopians hope that the change will eventually lead to a much better life for the country's people.

Chapter 2

THE LAND

In the northeastern region of the African continent there is a land bulge that juts out along the Red Sea into the Indian Ocean. This bulge is often called the "Horn" of Africa due to its shape. The country of Somalia occupies much of the Horn, as does eastern Ethiopia.

Ethiopia is one of the world's larger countries. Its 471,800 square miles (1,221,900 square kilometers) place it twenty-third in the world—about twice as big as the state of Texas.

The Red Sea borders Ethiopia on the northeast. The rather large country of Somalia and the small nation of Djibouti are to the east. Somalia and Kenya are to the south, and the Sudan, which is Africa's largest nation, lies to the west.

One reason why Ethiopia has played a key role in several major world events is its location. Ethiopia is close to the continent of Asia and trade routes to Egypt and the Persian Gulf. The Yemen Arab Republic is less than 50 miles (80 kilometers) across the long, narrow Red Sea. Southern Europe is only about 1,500 miles (2,400 kilometers) to the northwest of Ethiopia. Because of its closeness, Ethiopia traded spices, ivory, gold, frankincense, and slaves to nations from Asia and Europe, who in turn tried to conquer Ethiopia at various times.

The Simen Mountains in the northwest

Ethiopia is one of the most mountainous countries in Africa. About two-thirds of its land is comprised of mountainous regions and high plateaus. About one-third of the country is lowlands. For the most part, the lowlands form a fringe around Ethiopia's borders while the highlands occupy most of the interior.

Since ancient times, Ethiopians have thought of their country as having three kinds of land: the *qolla* refers to the lowlands; the *wayna dega* is the high plateau regions between 5,000 and 8,000 feet (1,500 to 2,400 meters) above sea level; and the *dega* refers to the mountainous areas that tower more than 8,000 feet (2,400 meters) above sea level.

The Simen Mountains in the northwest form the nation's highest range. Ethiopia's tallest peak—Ras Dashen—is located in the Simens. At 15,158 feet (4,620 meters) above sea level, Ras Dashen is the fourth tallest peak in Africa. The lowest spot, 381 feet (116 meters) below sea level, is in the Denakil Depression only a few hundred miles to the east, a large basin in northeast Ethiopia.

The Blue Nile Falls

RIVERS, LAKES, AND THE SEACOAST

All of Ethiopia's rivers begin in the country's highlands. The country's main river is the Blue Nile, which is one of the two main branches of the Nile, the world's longest river. The source of the Blue Nile is Lake Tana in the northwest. Flowing west out of Ethiopia, the Blue Nile enters the Sudan, where it and the White Nile merge at the city of Khartoum to become a single river called simply the Nile. Egypt, north of Ethiopia, has long depended on the Nile for providing fertile soil and irrigating the land. Eighty-three percent of the water and most of the silt arriving in Egypt comes from Ethiopia. Once they learned that the Blue Nile began in Ethiopia, the ancient Egyptians developed an almost supernatural fear that the Ethiopians would somehow stop the river's flow, thereby depriving Egypt of precious water. This fear has been true from ancient times to the present.

The Awash River (left) near the city of Nazaret
and hot springs of Lake Shala (right)

Other rivers include the Tekeze in the northwest; the Baro in the west; the Awash, which flows from central Ethiopia to the country's eastern border; and the Shebele in the southeast. One of Ethiopia's major problems is a poor transportation system within the country. Unfortunately, the Blue Nile and most of the other rivers in Ethiopia cannot be used much for transportation because of the steep gorges, waterfalls, and sharp twists and turns in their courses.

Lake Tana, covering about 1,400 square miles (3,627 square kilometers), is Ethiopia's largest lake. A series of lakes also occupies the Great Rift valley, which begins in the far north, cuts down the center of the country, and then stretches down Africa's east coast to the country of Mozambique. Among the beautiful lakes that fill up the hollows of the valley are the Rift Valley Lakes, which stretch like a string of blue jewels from the central to the southwestern part of the country. Another of the Great Rift

14

Left: *Papyrus boats on Lake Tana*
Right: *Fishing for small sharks off the Red Sea coast*

Valley Lakes—Lake Rudolf—is completely in Kenya except where it touches the southwestern Ethiopian border.

In the northeast, Ethiopia has a 628-mile (1,011-kilometer) seacoast along the Red Sea. The Dahlak Islands in the Red Sea, consisting of two larger islands and more than a hundred smaller ones, belong to Ethiopia.

CLIMATE

Because Ethiopia is close to the equator, there is not a tremendous difference in temperature in a given place from month to month. However, the climate varies greatly from place to place, with the variations mainly dependent on altitude. The lowest portions are generally the hottest, while the highest are the coolest.

The qolla take the form of rain forests, deserts, and grasslands.

*A view of the Great Rift valley (above) and sulfurous
springs (right), both in the Denakil Depression*

Temperatures in the lowlands often reach more than 90 degrees
Fahrenheit (32.2 degrees Celsius) during the day. In the Ogaden, a
desertlike region in the southeast, temperatures often top 100
degrees Fahrenheit (37.8 degrees Celsius). In the Denakil
Depression of northern Ethiopia, one of the hottest places on our
planet, the temperature sometimes reaches a broiling 120 degrees
Fahrenheit (48.9 degrees Celsius). In the town of Mitsiwa on the
Red Sea, the temperature also reaches 120 degrees Fahrenheit at
times.

The temperatures in the wayna dega are much more
comfortable—typically around 70 degrees Fahrenheit (21.1
degrees Celsius) during the day. Thanks to their moderate
temperatures, most cities and towns are located here. Lands in this
middle altitude are well suited to agriculture and cover about
two-thirds of the country.

The dega have temperatures ranging from a high of 60 degrees
Fahrenheit (15.6 degrees Celsius) in the day to as low as slightly

A sick mother brings her undernourished child (left) to a drought relief camp (right) during the mid-1980s famine.

below freezing at night. At the same moment that people in the lowlands are sweating from high temperatures, the mountains may be experiencing frost or hail.

Although temperatures do not vary greatly during the year, rainfall does. The rainy season (called *keremt*) lasts from mid-June through mid-September, while a season of small rains (called *belg*) lasts from March through May. The rest of the year is dry. The lowlands receive little rainfall—less than 8 inches (20.3 centimeters) yearly in many places. The mountains and plateaus receive much more—about 40 inches (101.6 centimeters) per year.

One of the country's great misfortunes is that its rainfall is not dependable. Many times droughts have killed cattle, crops, and ultimately people. One of the worst tragedies of the twentieth century struck Ethiopia and a number of other African countries during the mid-1980s when drought caused the deadliest famine ever recorded in Africa. At least 500,000 Africans died, almost half of them in Ethiopia.

Above: Gathering firewood near Bahar Dar   Right, clockwise from top: A spotted hyena, zebras, and a baboon with her baby

NATURAL RESOURCES

Ethiopia does not have abundant minerals, though gold has been mined in the south. The geothermal potential of the Great Rift Valley Lakes are being developed. In Ogaden, some petroleum has been found, but not in commercial quantities.

At the beginning of the twentieth century, about 40 percent of the land was covered with forests. This has been reduced to 4 percent. This affects materials needed in the building of houses and the availability of fuel for household use. But most important, the reduction of forestland has contributed to the problem of erosion.

Although many wild animals have been killed in recent years,

Clockwise from top left: A yellow-billed stork, a black and white colobus monkey, giraffes, flamingos, and African elephants

the country still has a great variety of wildlife. Hippopotamuses, rhinoceroses, crocodiles, and pythons live close to the rivers. Lions, elephants, giraffes, zebras, gazelles, and buffalo roam the country's protected parks and few forested areas. Ethiopia is home to special animals such as the mountain nyala and the walia ibex. A common kind of large monkey, the baboon, likes to steal farmers' crops. Another kind, the rare colobus monkey, was once killed for its lovely black and white fur, but is now protected by law. Hyenas, which are disliked for their weird howl and for their habit of eating dead things, still live in Ethiopia. Some of the world's widest variety of birds live in Ethiopia. Among the birds that can be found are ostriches, pelicans, flamingos, storks, egrets, ibises, larks, eagles, hawks, and vultures.

Chapter 3

HISTORY TO 1850

Researchers have found that basic language groups, including both Cushitic and Semitic languages that make up present-day Ethiopia, existed before outsiders arrived in Ethiopia. By the time migrants came from southern Arabia, the Cushitic people of the central highlands already were using the plow.

THE LAND OF PUNT

The ancient Egyptians called present-day Ethiopia and other lands along the Red Sea's southern border the Land of Punt. In about 2000 B.C., an Egyptian named Hennu sailed to the Land of Punt. The spot where Hennu landed is not known, but it may have been in Ethiopia. Over the next several hundred years, other Egyptians sailed to Ethiopia where they obtained human slaves, cattle, animal skins, and ivory.

Hundreds of years after the Egyptians began exploring the Land of Punt, the ancient Greeks named the region Ethiopia, meaning "Land of the Burnt Face." According to old Greek stories, the Ethiopians were dark because the sun-god, Apollo, approached too close to the ground and gave the people permanent suntans.

NEW PEOPLE ARRIVE

In about 1000 B.C., people from Arabia sailed south across the Red Sea and entered what is now northern Ethiopia. Some of these people became known as the *Habesha*. Abyssinia—an ancient name for Ethiopia that is still sometimes used—is thought to have evolved from the name Habesha.

The Habesha and other Arabian people brought an advanced civilization to Ethiopia. They possessed a written language and their architects and builders created lovely temples where the people worshiped such gods as the sun, the moon, and the planet Venus. Their farmers had the benefit of plows, dams, and irrigation ditches. These newcomers shared their culture with those who were already living in Ethiopia—sometimes through conquest and sometimes through marriage.

With the help of the people they conquered and married, the Habesha and other Arabians built an empire in the northern part of Ethiopia. According to Ethiopian tradition, the Old Testament's Queen of Sheba lived in this empire. Most of Ethiopia's emperors were said to have been descendants of the Queen of Sheba and Israel's King Solomon. However, some historians think that if there really was a Queen of Sheba, she lived across the Red Sea in Arabia.

THE AKSUMITE KINGDOM

By several hundred years before the birth of Christ, the descendants of Ethiopia's early people had built the Aksumite Kingdom in and around the town of Aksum (which is still inhabited) in northern Ethiopia. The Aksumite Kingdom had a

Above: Stelae *still standing at Aksum*
Below: A panoramic view of Aksum

Left: The old St. Mary of Zion Church in Aksum   Above: The new St. Mary of Zion Church with a fallen stele in front of it.

port city called Adulis on the Red Sea about 150 miles (240 kilometers) from Aksum. Merchants from Egypt, Greece, India, and other countries landed in Adulis, then traveled by caravan to Aksum, where they traded gold, silver, copper, ivory, spices, cotton, animal skins, jars, and glassware with the Aksumites. By about the year A.D. 50, the Aksumite Kingdom had become very wealthy and was well known in Egypt and Rome.

Many reminders of the powerful Aksumite Kingdom still stand in and around Aksum. In the third and fourth centuries, the Aksumite kings built over a hundred tall, thin stone monuments called *stelae*. The purpose of these skinny "skyscrapers" is unknown, but possibly they served as tombstones. The largest of the stelae was over one hundred feet (thirty meters) high and was probably the world's tallest monument at the time, but today it lies broken on the ground. The largest stela still standing is about seventy feet (twenty-one meters) high.

Stone thrones as well as palace ruins are also visible at Aksum, and a number of old coins from the Aksumite Kingdom have been unearthed. Some of these nearly two-thousand-year-old coins bear pictures of the crescent moon and a "star," which may represent the planet Venus.

Early in the fourth century, the Aksumite king Ezana was converted to Christianity. According to legend, the religion was said to have been introduced to Ethiopia by two young Syrians named Frumentius and Aedesius.

Frumentius and Aedesius were on a ship with their philosopher uncle in the Red Sea when pirates attacked. The uncle and everyone else except Frumentius and Aedesius were murdered. The boys somehow made it to the Ethiopian port of Adulis, and from there they were taken to Aksum. The king was so impressed by the youths that he named Frumentius his treasurer and Aedesius his cupbearer. After the king died, Frumentius and Aedesius helped the queen rule the country. They also tutored the young prince, Ezana, who became king in about A.D. 326.

Frumentius and Aedesius were devout Christians, and managed to convert many Ethiopians from their worship of heavenly bodies to Christianity. Coins made during the reign of King Ezana offer proof that many people really did convert to Christianity at this time. At the start of Ezana's reign, the coins show the old moon and "star" symbols. Later coins during Ezana's reign display the Christian cross. In fact, the coins from Ezana's reign are among the oldest ones displaying the Christian cross that have been found.

King Ezana was baptized into the Christian faith in about the year 340. Soon after, he began making inscriptions celebrating his adoption of Christianity. Unlike Rome, in Ethiopia the king became Christian first and then he converted the population. The newly-converted Ethiopians also began building Christian churches, the first of which may have been Saint Mary of Zion.

Frumentius traveled to Alexandria, Egypt, where he asked the famous Christian leader Athanasius to put someone in charge of the new converts at Aksum. Although Frumentius had not been trained for the priesthood, Athanasius named him to be the first leader of the Ethiopian church. For the next sixteen hundred years, the *abun* (archbishop) of the Ethiopian Orthodox church was appointed by the religious leader at Alexandria.

Gradually more and more Ethiopians were converted to Christianity, which by the sixth century was the country's leading religion. Northern Ethiopia's culture was molded by Christianity. Most literature, artwork, and music have focused on Christian themes. The country's churches and monasteries are its leading architectural landmarks, and for centuries Ethiopia's priests and monks were virtually the only educated people in the country.

Visitors to the city of Aksum began calling it one of the wonders of the world. In 525 a visitor named Cosmas said that the palace at Aksum had four towers topped with statues of unicorns, and that tame giraffes and elephants roamed the palace grounds. Another visitor said that the Aksumite king wore a gold-studded turban and jewelry made of gold, pearls, and precious stones, and that he traveled about on an elephant-drawn chariot. This was the golden age of the Aksumite Kingdom.

Early in the seventh century a new religion called Islam was founded by the prophet Muhammad in what is now Saudi Arabia, across the Red Sea from Ethiopia. When some Muslims (followers of the Islamic religion) were persecuted in Arabia, Muhammad advised them to flee to Ethiopia. At first the Ethiopian Christians welcomed them, but as the Muslims continued to pour into Ethiopia's coastal region, they came into conflict with the Christians. Several times the Ethiopians even crossed the Red Sea to make raids on the Muslims in Arabia.

With the Muslims taking control of Ethiopia's coast, the people

During the twelfth and thirteenth centuries,
King Lalibela ordered workers to carve churches
out of rock in the town bearing his name.
Remains of these churches can still be seen.

of the Aksumite Kingdom were not able to carry on the trade with
other countries that had made them wealthy. This was one reason
why the Aksumite Kingdom declined, starting in the seventh
century. Because of the breakdown of Red Sea trade, Ethiopia's
political power shifted gradually to the more fertile, productive
lands in the south.

THE ZAGWE DYNASTY

Ethiopia had no single ruling people for several hundred years
after the fall of the Aksumite Kingdom. Instead, each of the
country's many different groups of people was ruled by its own
king. Then during the early 1100s the Zagwe Dynasty began. It
was centered around the town of Lalibela (originally called Roha)
about 150 miles (240 kilometers) south of Aksum. Although the
Zagwe kings were also Christian, they did not claim the
Solomonic line. During the time (more than a century) the Zagwe

Left: An ancient crown from the church treasury of Aksum Right: Celebrating Christmas in the courtyard of one of the rockhewn churches in Lalibela

were Ethiopia's most powerful people, they built a series of beautiful churches dug out of solid rock.

Lalibela is in a mountainous region, and is not very far from Ethiopia's highest peak, Ras Dashen. During the late 1100s and early 1200s, the Zagwe King Lalibela ordered his workers to carve eleven churches out of the existing rock in the city that was named for him. The famous rock-hewn churches of Lalibela are still used today, nearly a thousand years after they were created. The Zagwe people also built other churches and monasteries in a large area around Lalibela.

The Zagwe Dynasty clashed with other groups, especially ones who wanted the descendants of Solomon and Sheba to once again rule Ethiopia. Between 1220 (the year Lalibela died) and 1270, the Zagwe were almost constantly at war. In 1270, Yekuno Amalak, a king claiming to be of the Solomonic line, took power, ending the Zagwe Dynasty.

THE AMHARA AND TIGRAY PEOPLE

Yekuno Amalak was a member of the Amhara, a people who lived in the Amhara region north of the center of Ethiopia. The Amhara, and also the Tigray people who lived north of them, were descendants of the local people and those who had come from Arabia. For many hundreds of years, the Amhara, and to a lesser extent the Tigray, dominated most aspects of Ethiopian political life, but drew much of their vocabulary, religious ideas, and technology from people they lived with or conquered.

The Amhara and Tigray have held most of Ethiopia's key political positions during the past thousand years. An ancient language called Ge'ez, spoken by the Amhara and Tigray, became the language of the Ethiopian church and of many of the country's authors. The Amharic language, a sister language of Ge'ez evolved separately many hundreds of years ago and became the official language of Ethiopia's government, schools, and courts.

EMPERORS AND KINGS

By about the 1200s the man who ruled over all of Ethiopia was known as the *negusa nagast*, meaning "king of kings." In English this person is usually called the emperor. Under the emperor were a number of regional kings, each of whom was called a *negus*, and lesser regional lords known as *rases*.

Farmers had to pay a portion of their crops and livestock to their king as a tribute, or tax. They produced enough grain to support a wealthy nobility. The farmers also had to fight for their king if need be. In turn, each king had to pay tributes of livestock, cloth, and gold to the emperor, and help him raise armies. Ethiopia's rulers amassed the food, materials, and labor to support their court from these tributes.

Until the sixteenth century, emperors generally did not live in one place, but instead spent their lives moving about the country. Wherever the emperor was located at any given time was considered Ethiopia's capital.

As the emperor and his followers moved about, tents served as their movable homes, churches, and storehouses. The emperor, who was highly revered, spent most of his time behind curtains, and when he came out in public people were supposed to avoid looking at his face. The subjects of one emperor, Zara Yakob, kissed the ground whenever he spoke. When traveling, the emperor sat in a curtained chair carried by his assistants. A man with a cross and another with a bell headed the procession to warn people off the road. Accompanying the procession were the emperor's large livestock herds and chained lions, which symbolized his great power.

Ethiopia has always been a war-torn country, and even in recent years it has been the scene of many terrible battles.

Unusually the fighting was between Ethiopians, rather than against another country. The kings often sent their private armies against one another as they vied for power. Besides vying for power, emperors and kings wanted to expand south where wealth could be had through gold and slavery, and later, coffee and hides. These goods could be traded on the world market.

Often family members coveted the throne enough to murder for it. To stop this, many emperors kept the royal relatives on *ambas*, flat-topped mountains, where they lived freely and well but could not leave. When an emperor or king died, many people claimed his title—very often based on legitimate descent. However, it was always the most powerful who assumed the title.

EUROPEANS ARRIVE

Ever since the days of the ancient Greeks, Ethiopia had been a place of mystery to Europeans. During the 1300s, a strange story circulated through Europe about a powerful Christian priest-king in Ethiopia named Prester John. There really *was* a powerful Christian emperor in Ethiopia, but this imaginary Prester John was supposed to be almost superhuman. He reportedly ruled over seventy-two kings in a land far larger than Ethiopia, and his mighty army was said to be capable of defeating the Muslims who were then taking over much of Europe and Asia. The Prester John legend attracted some Europeans to Ethiopia, which enabled the country to obtain European help against some of its enemies.

During the late 1400s, a few Portuguese and other Europeans came to Ethiopia seeking Prester John's aid in fighting the Muslims. In 1520, while Lebna Dengel was emperor, the king of Portugal sent some ambassadors to Ethiopia. With them was Father Francisco Alvarez, who later wrote *True Information on the Lands of Prester John*, a book that has provided a great deal of information about sixteenth-century Ethiopia.

But within Ethiopia lived many different people—not all of whom accepted Christianity or the emperor's authority. Beginning in 1527, the Muslim leader Ahmed ibn Ibrahim al-Ghazi and his forces attacked northern Ethiopia. The Ethiopians referred to Ahmed as *gran*, meaning "left-handed." For sixteen years, Ahmed Gran and his forces, which included some soldiers from Turkey with firearms, conquered Christian Ethiopia and burned churches and monasteries. They even stormed a fortress atop Amba Gishen and murdered the imprisoned members of the royal family. During this period many Ethiopians converted to Islam and their descendants have held to that religion.

Remembering that the Portuguese had sought help against the Muslims, Emperor Lebna Dengel sent a message to the king of Portugal asking his help in fighting Ahmed Gran. In 1541, the year after Lebna Dengel died, a four-hundred-man Portuguese army arrived in Ethiopia. At its head was Christopher da Gama, son of the famed explorer Vasco da Gama who had led the first European expedition to reach India by sea.

The Portuguese army planned to join with the forces of the new emperor, Galawdewos, son of Lebna Dengal. Before they could do that, Christopher da Gama was captured and killed by Ahmed Gran's forces in the summer of 1542. About two hundred of his men also were killed in several battles.

Thinking total victory was his, Ahmed Gran retired with his men to his headquarters near Lake Tana. In late 1542, however, the remaining Portuguese army combined with Emperor Galawdewos's forces. They marched to Lake Tana, and in the battle fought there in early 1543 Ahmed Gran and many of his men were killed. The rest of Ahmed Gran's army then scattered.

Galawdewos soon recaptured his kingdom, rebuilding many of the churches that the Muslims had burned. Some of Ahmed Gran's soldiers remained in Ethiopia, where they joined the Muslims who had been living in the country for many generations. The Portuguese soldiers also remained in Ethiopia, marrying Ethiopian women and adding yet another group to the blend of the many people who live in the country.

In the early sixteenth century, the Oromo people migrated from

Lake Awasa in the Rift valley

the southern Rift valley region and spread to most of Ethiopia as far north as Eritrea and around Lake Tana. The Oromo were excellent horsemen and many became soldiers at the imperial capital at Gondar. Many others settled and became farmers. Today they are Ethiopia's largest single ethnic language group. Ethiopia's culture, history, and language have been enriched by the Oromo.

Meanwhile, people in Portugal and Spain were hoping that the Ethiopians could be persuaded to abandon the Ethiopian Orthodox church and become Roman Catholics. Between 1550 and 1630, Portuguese and Spanish missionaries came to Ethiopia, where they worked to convert the people to Roman Catholicism.

The Emperor Susenyos, who reigned between 1607 and 1632, converted to Roman Catholicism, and then he and the Roman Catholic missionaries also tried to force other Ethiopians to convert. Some did this willingly, others went along with it to save their lives, but still others resisted, including sixty monks who chose to leap off a cliff rather than renounce the Ethiopian

Orthodox religion. During the early 1600s, a civil war was fought between Emperor Susenyos's forces and those who refused to give up their faith.

During one terrible battle, Susenyos's forces killed several thousand Ethiopians who had refused to renounce their religion. Gazing at the bodies on the battlefield, Emperor Susenyos's son, Fasilidas, said, "The men you see strewn upon the earth were your own subjects, your compatriots, some of them your kinsmen. . . . This is no victory that we have gained."

Sickened by all the bloodshed, Susenyos gave in to the pleas of his son and many thousands of other Ethiopians. In June of 1632 he issued this proclamation:

> Originally we gave you the Roman faith thinking it to
> be a good one. But countless men because of it have
> gone to their death: Yolyos, Gabriel, Takla-Giyorgis, and
> now a multitude of peasants. Now therefore we restore
> to you the Faith of your ancestors. Let the clergy return
> to the churches and set up their own altars for the
> Sacrament; let the people follow their own Liturgy, and
> may their hearts be glad!

That same year Susenyos gave up the throne in favor of his son, Fasilidas, and the Roman Catholic missionaries were soon expelled from the country.

Emperor Fasilidas decided to build a permanent capital at Gondar, north of Lake Tana in the northwest. At Gondar, he and several kings built beautiful stone palaces, as well as churches. Fasilidas's reign lasted thirty-five years, until 1667. According to some sources, he actually died in 1662, but his death was kept secret for five years because of disagreements over who should become the next emperor.

The imperial compound at Gondar

During the late 1700s, the power of the emperor diminished. One reason for this was that, with the emperor at Gondar most of the time, the regional kings could be more aggressive. Also, because of the tributes the kings received, outside trade stagnated. Between the late 1600s and the mid-1800s the regional kings often fought over power. At one time, in about 1800, six different men were vying to become emperor. This period, which lasted for more than a century, is called the "Age of the Princes" because each region had its own supreme ruler and was like a little country of its own. Then, during the 1850s, a strong emperor took control of Ethiopia—but with what proved to be tragic results.

Chapter 4

FROM 1850 TO 1945

EMPEROR TEWODROS II

Many major changes in Ethiopia have been brought about by powerful men who exerted their control by force. The "Age of the Princes" was ended by such a man: Emperor Tewodros II, who came to power in 1855.

Tewodros worked to improve his country, especially in his first years as emperor. He announced that people could appeal to him directly as the country's supreme judge, and kept his promise by listening to legal cases for hours each day. He ended the custom of killing the relatives of murderers, and imposed harsh penalties for thievery. For centuries some non-Christian Ethiopians as well as some members of several other groups had been enslaved by the Amhara, Tigray, and other ruling people. Tewodros tried, unsuccessfully, to end slavery.

Realizing that the regional kings would be more likely to challenge him if he stayed in one place, Tewodros announced, "I shall build no capital city. My tent—wherever it stands—will be my capital." Although Tewodros spent a great deal of time at Amba Mekdala, the flat-topped mountain east of Lake Tana, he did roam the countryside and live in a tent the same as the emperors of old.

Emperor Tewodros (left) and Yohannes (above)

Emperor Tewodros stripped numerous governors and judges of their power, and replaced them with his own men. He imprisoned those who might pose a threat to him, including a youth named Sahle Mariam, who escaped and later became Emperor Menilek II.

Many European missionaries and travelers entered Ethiopia during Tewodros's reign. Tewodros became enchanted with Europe. He reorganized Ethiopia's army along European lines, and hired European craftsmen to build weapons.

But after his wife and two of his English friends died, Tewodros turned into a cruel tyrant who treated his enemies harshly. At this time Europeans were vying to gain control of eastern Africa. Tewodros tried to establish good foreign relations, but had a misunderstanding with the British. A well-equipped British army arrived at the gates of Mekdela, and rather than fall into British hands, Tewodros committed suicide in 1868.

YOHANNES IV

After Tewodros's death, there were more civil wars to determine who would be emperor. Tigray Yohannes IV won, partly because he had some arms left by the British after they had retreated. Yohannes soon faced problems both from within and from outside his country. His main internal problem was a powerful regional king named Menilek of Shewa Province who wanted to become emperor. Their dispute was settled in 1882 when Emperor Yohannes and Menilek made a deal. Yohannes took control of the more important (at the time) northern half of the country, while Menilek took control of his home area of Shewa.

Ethiopia was threatened also by other nations during the reign of Yohannes IV. In 1869 the Suez Canal opened in eastern Egypt, connecting the Mediterranean Sea to the Red Sea. The Suez Canal made it easier for European ships to reach Ethiopia and many other countries in Africa and Asia. It helped European countries in their colonization efforts in Africa and Asia.

It was soon evident that Great Britain, Italy, and France all had their eyes on Ethiopia. In 1869, an Italian shipping company bought the Ethiopian port town of Assab on the Red Sea from a local ruler. The Italian government then took control of Assab from the shipping company. During the 1880s, the Italians also tried to take over inland areas of Ethiopia. In 1887 Ethiopian forces beat the Italians at the battle of Dogali in the far northern part of the country, forcing the Italians to retreat.

Yohannes also had to defeat the Egyptians several times, and in 1887 Muslims from the Sudan also invaded. The Ethiopians did well in some battles against the Sudanese, but in the spring of 1889 Yohannes was killed in the fighting.

Emperor Menilek II

MENILEK II

Following Yohannes's death in 1889, Menilek II was crowned emperor. In 1887, while king of Shewa Province, Menilek and his empress Taitu had founded the city of Addis Ababa near the center of Ethiopia. When Menilek II became emperor in 1889, Addis Ababa became capital of the entire country, as it still is. As part of his foreign policy, Menilek played the European powers against one another.

Menilek set out to conquer the south in order to have access to ivory, slaves, gold, and other forms of tribute that enabled him to buy arms. He conquered the lands of the Oromo, the Kingdom of Kafa, the town of Harar, and Sidama ethnic areas that produced commodities.

Also in the year he became emperor, Menilek made a treaty with Italy, who was then taking control of Eritrea, a northern province. This treaty granted Italy part of Eritrea. In return, Italy gave Ethiopia money, thousands of rifles, and several dozen cannons.

Menilek went to war with Italy due to an argument over a word in the 1889 treaty. In the Ethiopian version of the treaty, it said that the emperor *could* ask the Italians for help if Ethiopia had trouble with its foreign affairs. In the Italian version, it said that the emperor *must* ask the Italians for help regarding its foreign affairs.

There is a big difference between "could" and "must." Ethiopian leaders thought they had the choice of seeking help from Italy if they wanted. But the Italians considered themselves in charge of all of Ethiopia's foreign affairs, meaning that Ethiopia had become a protectorate of Italy.

When they learned about the Italian version, and as Italian forces marched farther into their territory, Ethiopians realized the truth. Italy's true goal was to control all of Ethiopia. The emperor renounced the treaty in May of 1893.

At this time, most of Africa was ruled by European countries. Except for France and Russia, the nations of Europe recognized Italy's right to govern Ethiopia's foreign affairs. Great Britain, which ruled a large number of colonies in many parts of the world, said that Italy could do what it pleased in Ethiopia as long as it did not interfere in Egypt, which was then coming under British control.

In preparation for a fight with Italy, Menilek obtained weapons from France and Russia. In 1895 the Italians invaded Tigray Province, just south of Eritrea. Menilek asked the regional leaders to help him fight the Italians and gathered an army of 120,000 men. Facing them was an Italian force of 20,000 men, about half of

The Battle of Adowa

them troops from Eritrea. Although fewer in number, the Italians had modern weapons, while many of the Ethiopians were armed only with spears. But Menilek also had modern rifles and artillery provided by Italy in 1889.

The two armies met at Adowa, in Tigray Province in northern Ethiopia, on March 1, 1896. The Ethiopians inflicted a crushing defeat on the Italians. Exact figures are not known, but it is thought that about twelve thousand men died in the Battle of Adowa, most of them on the Italian side.

The Ethiopians had beaten the Italians in a lesser battle in 1887, at Dogali, but the great victory at Adowa in 1896 marked one of the first times that an African nation defeated a European nation in a major battle. After this, Italy was forced to recognize Ethiopia's independence, except for the Eritrea area. Had he done nothing else, Menilek would be remembered as a hero for keeping his country independent at a time when Europeans were colonizing Africa. For by the early 1900s, only two African countries, Ethiopia and Liberia, were independent. All the others had been carved up among Great Britain, France, Germany, Portugal, Italy, Belgium, and Spain.

Yet Menilek was willing to make deals with European powers, if Ethiopia could profit by them. For example, France, which controlled the little country of Djibouti to the northeast, wanted to build a railroad from Addis Ababa to the city of Djibouti. Menilek gave his permission, and so, between 1894 and 1917, the French built Ethiopia's first railroad, a 500-mile (804-kilometer) line that benefited both France and Ethiopia. Addis Ababa now became the chief commercial city for the export of coffee, hides, and other goods from the rich southern provinces.

Menilek II helped modernize Ethiopia in many other ways. He helped found the country's first public school, bank, and postal service. He helped bring the telegraph, telephone, and electricity to parts of Ethiopia. And he led the first public health efforts by organizing a campaign to vaccinate Ethiopians against disease.

EMPRESS ZAWDITU

After serving as emperor for about a quarter of a century, Menilek II died in 1913, having named his grandson, Lij Iyasu, to succeed him. But the teenaged Lij Iyasu was young and impetuous and offended the old elite. The dominant Christian sector was upset also that Lij Iyasu seemed to favor the Muslim religion. Some historians feel that Iyasu really wanted to create a nonsectarian Ethiopia. In 1916 Lij Iyasu was overthrown by leaders of the Ethiopian Orthodox church, the army, and the country's noblemen.

Zawditu, Menilek's daughter, then became empress in 1917. It was against Ethiopian law for a woman to rule the country by herself, so Ras (Prince) Tafari Makonnen (the son of Menilek's cousin) was named regent to the empress. Ras Tafari was so forceful, intelligent, and politically shrewd that he was expected to one day become emperor, which occurred thirteen years later when he was crowned Emperor Haile Sellassie I.

HAILE SELLASSIE I

Ras Tafari worked to have Ethiopia admitted to the League of Nations, the international organization that was the forerunner to the United Nations. In 1919 Ethiopia was refused admission to the League, partly because the country still had slavery. But in 1923 Ras Tafari and Empress Zawditu issued an edict outlawing slavery and the slave trade and Ethiopia was admitted to the League that same year. During the next several years, the government passed laws providing for the freeing of existing slaves.

In 1930, Ras Tafari Makonnen became emperor after defeating Ras Gugsa, Zawditu's former husband, in a battle in the north, and the death of Zawditu. He took the name Haile Sellassie, which means "power of the trinity."

Haile Sellassie granted Ethiopia its first constitution in the summer of 1931. But instead of giving more power to the people, the constitution made certain that the bulk of the power remained with the emperor and the nobility. For example, although the constitution created a two-house assembly, its members were appointed by the emperor from among the nobility rather than elected by the people. Haile Sellassie also appointed men loyal to

A 1930 photo of Haile Sellassie with his family

him as regional rulers. In effect, Haile Sellassie was in charge of all aspects of Ethiopian political life — the central and local governments and the courts. And just as had been the case for many generations, the Amhara and the Tigray were appointed to most of the government positions, while many other groups, especially southern people, were generally ignored.

As emperor, Haile Sellassie continued to slowly expand Ethiopia's school, health, and communication systems. He oversaw the creation of newspapers, although he forbade them to criticize him. And, during one of Ethiopia's most difficult times in its long history, Haile Sellassie proved to be his country's savior.

ITALY'S INVASION

Although defeated at Adowa in 1896, Italy still ruled Eritrea, in what is now northern Ethiopia. Despite a twenty-year treaty of friendship that it had signed with Ethiopia in 1928, Italy made plans to conquer Ethiopia during the 1930s. Benito Mussolini, Italy's ruler, thought that crops to feed a vast Italian empire could be grown in Ethiopia. The Italians also wanted to avenge their defeat at Adowa.

On December 5, 1934, Ethiopian and Italian troops battled at Wal Wal in the Ogaden Desert along the border with Somalia where the Italians had built a fort. It is not known how it began, but it is known that about a hundred Ethiopians and about thirty Italians were killed in this battle. The Italians complained to the League of Nations that the Ethiopians had attacked their property without cause. The Ethiopians said that Wal Wal was theirs.

In looking back, it seems that Ethiopia was in the right regarding this dispute. But at the time, Great Britain, France, and some other nations were afraid of getting into a war against Italy and Germany. For that reason, they did not condemn Italy for its actions against Ethiopia. Italy realized that it could probably get away with doing whatever it wanted. Using Eritrea as their military base, the Italians then invaded Ethiopia in October 1935.

Haile Sellassie gathered an army that included sections of the modern army, the old imperial army, farmers, rases, and local militia. It was a one-sided fight, however. Barefoot and armed with old rifles or spears, the soldiers were no match for the airplanes, bombs, and poison gas of the Italians. Town after town fell to the enemy, and many thousands of Ethiopians were killed.

Haile Sellassie led the fight against Italy for several months, but it soon became obvious that the emperor could do more for his country in exile than by getting himself killed. On May 2, 1936, Haile Sellassie and his family left Addis Ababa, barely escaping capture by the Italians.

The Italians seized Addis Ababa on May 5 and four days later

Haile Sellassie ordered the mobilization of an army in 1935.

claimed possession of all Ethiopia. On June 1 they combined Ethiopia, Eritrea, and the Italian portion of Somalia and named their territory Italian East Africa. However, so much of Ethiopia remained independent of Italy that the country couldn't be said to have been colonized. The Italians emphasized the religious and ethnic differences to cause dissension among the occupied people.

Meanwhile, the emperor and his family went by train to Djibouti and soon traveled to London, England. Because the British were still afraid of angering Italy, they greeted Haile Sellassie coolly in London.

On June 30, 1936, Emperor Haile Sellassie went to the League of Nations headquarters in Geneva, Switzerland, where he made one of the most famous speeches of the twentieth century. "I, Haile Sellassie I, Emperor of Ethiopia, am here today to claim the justice which is due to my people," began the tired-looking emperor.

Left: Haile Sellassie in Paris on his way to talk before the League of Nations in Geneva, Switzerland
Right: In February 1937, Ethiopians tried to kill the Italian, Marshal Rodolfo Graziani.

After relating how the Italians had slaughtered his people by the "tens of thousands," he said that the League of Nations must protect the rights of less-powerful countries, because "apart from the Kingdom of the Lord there is not on this earth any nation which is superior to any other." At the end of his speech he said:

> God and history will remember your judgment. . . .Does this initiative mean the abandonment of Ethiopia to her aggressor? . . . I declare in the face of the whole world that the emperor, the government, and the people of Ethiopia will not bow before force. . . . I ask the fifty-two nations, who have given the Ethiopian people a promise to help them in their resistance to the aggressor, what are they willing to do for Ethiopia?. . . Representatives

of the world, I have come to Geneva to discharge in
your midst the most painful of the duties of the head of
a state. What reply have I to take back to my people?
Although newspapers throughout the world praised the
emperor as the conscience of humanity, the League of Nations
failed to help Ethiopia.

ETHIOPIAN RESISTANCE

There is still controversy over whether Haile Sellassie should
have left Ethiopia. But, even with their emperor gone, Ethiopians
continued to fight the invaders. Many patriotic Ethiopians, called
arbagna, stayed behind to organize resistance fighters.

In February of 1937, Ethiopians tried to kill Marshal Rodolfo
Graziani, commander of Italian forces in Ethiopia. In punishment,
the Italians executed about thirty thousand Ethiopians.

WORLD WAR II

Once the war began, British lawmakers decided to help the
Ethiopians drive out the Italians. In January of 1941 Emperor
Haile Sellassie returned to Ethiopia with not only British troops
but also Ethiopian soldiers who had taken refuge in Kenya and
Sudan. The British and Ethiopian forces gradually pushed the
Italians out. On May 5, 1941—almost exactly five years after he
had fled the capital—Haile Sellassie returned to Addis Ababa.

By 1945 World War II was over, with Ethiopia and the other
Allies triumphant. Many Italians stayed in Ethiopia to help build
the country as doctors, engineers, mechanics, farmers, and
laborers.

Chapter 5

FROM 1945 TO TODAY

THE ERITREAN QUESTION

The British, the Sudanese, and the Ethiopian partisans helped liberate Ethiopia. But Eritrea was thought of as a conquered Italian colony and had been occupied by the British between 1941 and 1945. After the end of World War II, Eritrea was under the United Nations. In 1952 the United Nations held a plebicite and Eritrea voted to join Ethiopia in a federated status, keeping its own Parliament.

DISSATISFACTION WITH HAILE SELLASSIE

Haile Sellassie dealt well with several crises just before and after World War II, but in rebuilding Ethiopia he created dissension with the majority of the people. In return for financial aid that it provided Ethiopia, Great Britain made some efforts to control Ethiopia's affairs. But Haile Sellassie stood firm about keeping his country independent, and just before World War II ended, Britain and Ethiopia signed an agreement in which they recognized one another as "equal and independent powers."

Mainly because of its failure to protect Ethiopia from Italian aggression at the start of World War II, the League of Nations disbanded at the end of the war. It was replaced by the United Nations in 1945. Ethiopia was one of the original members of the United Nations.

Haile Sellassie continued to gradually modernize Ethiopia after the war. He ordered new roads and schools built. He also worked to centralize the government—constantly taking power away from the regional rulers and giving it to lawmakers who were loyal to himself. In addition, he tried to give the country's diverse people a sense of unity. One way he did this was by making Amharic the national language and ordering that, wherever possible, schoolchildren be taught in Amharic.

The Non-Amhara people felt they were being excluded—politically and economically. Also many city dwellers felt too many privileges were being given to the nobility. Students, taxi drivers, teachers, and soldiers began to express their dissent. Many were angry that the Amhara, who comprised about 20 percent of the population, dominated political life. The Muslims, comprising almost half of the population, were rarely appointed to government positions. Many people objected to the fact that, of the seventy languages spoken in Ethiopia, Amharic was the one official language. Many people also were disgusted that the Addis Ababa region benefited most from the modernization drive, and that as a whole Ethiopia had one of the lowest standards of living. And although Haile Sellassie was clearly trying to improve life in Ethiopia, many thought that his pace was much too slow.

There were periodic signs of trouble. Regional leaders who resented the emperor for taking away their power led rebellions from time to time. As early as 1943, there was an armed rebellion in Tigray Province. But the first major sign occurred in 1960.

REVOLUTION

In December of that year, while Haile Sellassie was in Brazil, a group of idealistic army officers from the emperor's Imperial Bodyguard tried to seize control of the government. The attempted takeover was supported by a large number of university students in Addis Ababa. The rebels seized the Imperial Palace, where they imprisoned twenty-one important government ministers and officials who for the most part had been loyal to the emperor. The emperor's son, Crown Prince Asfa Wossen, was named by the rebels to head a new government. The prince read messages over the rebel-held radio station in which he spoke of "corruption in the government" and the "selfish people" who ran the country. However, it is thought that the rebels forced the prince to say these things. Had the prince refused, the rebels might have executed him.

The emperor learned what was occurring and returned to Ethiopia on December 16. Meanwhile, Ethiopia's army and air force, who had for the most part remained loyal to the emperor, were attacking rebel strongholds with tanks and airplanes. After heavy fighting in Ethiopia's capital city, the rebellion was crushed by December 17. The rebels executed fifteen of their prisoners and several of the rebel leaders shot themselves to avoid capture.

The main leaders of the rebellion were two brothers, Mengistu and Girmame Neway. Girmame Neway shot Mengistu to keep him from being captured, then killed himself with the same gun. Mengistu recovered, but was condemned to be hanged in public. Before that grisly sentence was carried out, Mengistu Neway made a speech in which he predicted that the emperor would soon be overthrown.

An officer of the Eritrean Liberation Front lectures his troops.

Several hundred people died during the 1960 revolt, and nearly a thousand were wounded. The emperor placed thousands of the rebels under arrest and also removed many government officials whom he considered disloyal.

Starting in the 1960s, Haile Sellassie also had to deal with groups that wanted several of Ethiopia's regions to separate from the country. Eritrea, which had a large Muslim population, became a major trouble spot. In 1962, the emperor ignored Eritrea's independent status and joined it to Ethiopia as Eritrea Province. Several organizations, including the Eritrean Liberation Front (ELF), were formed by Eritreans who wanted to separate their province from Ethiopia. During the 1960s and the 1970s, there were many battles between Ethiopian troops and the Eritrean rebels.

The Ogaden Desert became another trouble spot. In 1960 the country of Somalia gained its independence from Great Britain and Italy. The Somali people were for the most part nomads who traveled about with their herds of cattle, camels, goats, and sheep.

About a million of the Somalis lived in Ethiopia's Ogaden Desert, beyond the border of Somalia. Many of these people wanted part of the Ogaden to become part of Somalia. Starting in the early 1960s, there were battles between Ethiopian forces and Somali rebels in the Ogaden.

On top of all the political turmoil, Ethiopia was struck by a terrible natural disaster during the early 1970s. Ethiopia has always suffered from periodic famines caused by drought, but food production had been declining for many years. Between 1972 and 1974 a drought-caused famine killed several hundred thousand Ethiopians, most of them in Tigray and Welo provinces. Not only did Haile Sellassie's government fail to prevent this famine or help the victims, it also tried to cover up the disaster. To this day, little is known outside Ethiopia about this famine.

Dissatisfaction with the emperor's slow method of advancing the country, combined with his poor handling of the famine, contributed to his downfall. The elderly Haile Sellassie rapidly lost control of the country during the early 1970s. Numerous demonstrations were held to protest Haile Sellassie's rule. The army, seeking higher pay, turned against the emperor. And a growing number of university students and intellectuals blamed him for the country's low standard of living. The emperor was under such widespread attack that eventually he could no longer censor the media, who openly criticized him.

In the mid-1970s a movement began to free Tigray Province from Ethiopian rule. And in a large region south of Addis Ababa, the Oromo people (also called the Gallas), who resented Amhara rule formed the Oromo Liberation Front, which hoped to create an independent "People's Democratic Republic of Oromo" right inside Ethiopia.

Haile Sellassie (left) was arrested in 1974 and succeeded by Mengistu Haile Mariam (right).

HAILE SELLASSIE IS OVERTHROWN

In September of 1974, after forty-four years as emperor, Haile Sellassie was deposed. This marked the end of several thousand years of rule by Ethiopia's emperors, Haile Sellassie was placed under arrest in Addis Ababa, where a year later he died of natural causes at the age of eighty-three.

Although Haile Sellassie's regime collapsed without open fighting, soon a great amount of blood was being shed as rivals fought to control Ethiopia's government. A group of military leaders called the *dergue* (meaning "committee" in Amharic) emerged in control of Ethiopia. And a military officer named Mengistu Haile Mariam emerged as the leader of the dergue.

Mengistu Haile Mariam and his supporters adopted a slogan — *Ethiopia Tikdem*, meaning "Ethiopia First." This meant that they wanted the country as a whole to come before the interests of a few people. Soon, when they decided to make Ethiopia a Socialist country, they changed the motto to *Ye-Itiopia Hibretesebawinet*, meaning "Ethiopian Socialism."

In setting up a Socialist society, Mengistu Haile Mariam and his supporters proved to be as ruthless as Ethiopia's worst emperors. In 1977-78, during a period known as the "Red Terror Campaign," two factions trying to control the government struggled for power. Approximately thirty thousand Ethiopians who opposed the new government were killed. During the month of December 1977, as many as one thousand students in Addis Ababa were killed while passing out printed materials critical of the new military government. Thousands of people who objected to the new form of government and to its leaders were executed, and thousands more were placed in jails and concentration camps.

The new government, like the old, had problems with the Eritreans, Somalis, and Oromo who wanted to establish their own Independent states or to have better access to power within Ethiopia.

From 1953 until the time of the revolution, the United States had supplied Ethiopia with most of its weapons, and with money to improve conditions in the country. In 1977, the Somalis attacked Ethiopia, but because of human rights violations by the military government, the United States refused military support. Ethiopia turned against the United States and accepted aid from the Soviet Union. The Soviets then became Ethiopia's main supplier of military aid. In 1978, weapons and soldiers supplied by the Soviet Union and Cuba enabled Ethiopian forces to inflict a major defeat on the Somalis. But the Somalis, Eritreans, and other rebels continued fighting.

Just several years after a famine had helped to topple Haile Sellassie, the new government faced an even worse famine. During the early 1980s, the rainfall over a large region of Africa

A British Red Cross worker with famine victims in 1984

that included Ethiopia was below normal. Crops withered and livestock died of thirst. Soon people were dying by the thousands every day in Ethiopia and several other African countries.

FAMINE

Ethiopia was the hardest hit of all African countries. Relief workers who went to Ethiopia reported that people, who looked more like skeletons than human beings, were wandering about the countryside in search of food. Within a three-month period in late 1984, several hundred thousand Ethiopians died of hunger and its accompanying diseases. One big problem in getting help to the famine victims was that Ethiopia has very poor roads (partly due to the mountains and partly due to poverty), and that many rural people live many miles from any road at all.

Other problems also contributed to the famine. The civil war in

Eritrea and Tigray provinces disrupted the delivery of relief food to the victims. There is antagonism between the West and Ethiopia's Socialist regime, so Western aid agencies were slow to respond because they did not believe the government claims about the famine. Also, at that time, the Ethiopian government in Addis Ababa was spending several million dollars to celebrate the tenth anniversary of its having come to power.

Again in 1988, Ethiopia suffered another famine, caused by drought, civil war in Eritrea and Tigray provinces, and inappropriate agricultural policies.

A NEW GOVERNMENT

Despite the tragedy of the famine, and even despite all the deaths due to the political turmoil of the 1970s, many observers say that the new Socialist regime has done much good for Ethiopia. One of the new regime's main goals has been to create more schools in Ethiopia. Because they can produce teachers, doctors, and educated farmers that the country so desperately needs, schools are crucial to the country's future. Thus far hundreds of new schools have been built, along with roads, health clinics, and electric facilities.

These educational efforts have begun to pay off. Ethiopia's literacy race has been steadily climbing. In the early 1970s, less than ten Ethiopians in a hundred could read and write. As of 1987, it was estimated that about one in five could read and write.

The new government also has made a strong effort to help the nation's farmers, who comprise about 80 percent of the population. In the past, wealthy landlords owned much of the farmland. After the revolution, the Socialist government seized

Students in a mission school

the land, and distributed it to the farmers themselves. No longer did people have to work for and pay taxes to landlords. No longer did any individual own a tremendous amount of land. The government also organized cooperative associations to help farmers produce more goods and market them better. There were many violent clashes as the former landlords objected when their lands were seized and passed out to their former tenants.

Many large, privately owned farms also have been changed to state farms. The majority of the government's investment in agriculture goes to these state farms, even though 90 percent of all agricultural products are produced by small farmers. State farms have not been successful. Many experts in Ethiopia and outside have recommended that the government invest more in small, family-size farms.

Ethiopia still has many problems. Poverty, illiteracy, hunger, and disease still plague the ancient nation. It will take many years for the Socialist government—or for any future forms of government that may replace it—to make significant progress toward conquering these problems.

The Parliament building in Addis Ababa, now headquarters of the Workers' Party of Ethiopia

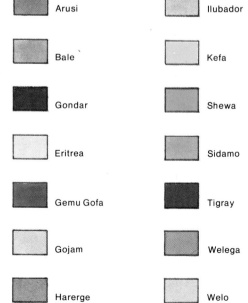

ADMINISTRATIVE DISTRICTS

Arusi

Bale

Gondar

Eritrea

Gemu Gofa

Gojam

Harerge

Ilubador

Kefa

Shewa

Sidamo

Tigray

Welega

Welo

Chapter 6

GOVERNMENT

Ethiopia's flag is rectangular in shape. On the flag there are three horizontal stripes that are equal in size—green, yellow, and red—from top to bottom.

Under Mengistu's rule the country has changed from control by a military council called a dergue to a one-party state led by the Workers' Party of Ethiopia (WPE). A new constitution was announced in 1987. Mengistu serves as president of the country and all offices are held by party members. Mengistu also oversees the appointment of officials to head the country's fourteen provinces, also called administrative divisions: Arusi, Bale, Gondar, Eritrea, Gemu Gofa, Gojam, Harerge, Ilubabor, Kefa, Shewa, Sidamo, Tigray, Welega, and Welo.

The government itself, rather than individuals, controls the land and factories. Besides overseeing land distribution, the government controls banks, insurance companies, transportation, newspapers, radio, and TV. The government also has taken over many manufacturing companies that were once privately owned. But private merchants are still important for distributing goods and most farmers still own their own animals and can decide how they will use their land.

A traditional homestead

A change occurred in the national government in the fall of 1987. Mengistu allowed the country to have an elected legislature, called the *National Shengo*. But Mengistu retained much of his power and it is questionable as to whether the people really have a voice in their government.

Despite Mengistu's tight control of the national government, he has provided people with more of a voice in their local affairs than previously. In farm areas there are thousands of peasant associations. Composed of dozens or even hundreds of families, each peasant association works to improve the way of life for its members. The peasant associations serve as local courts, are involved in collecting taxes and organizing military forces, and oversee health care and education for their people.

In 1985, the government ordered farmers to destroy their old houses that are scattered around the countryside and build new homes in villages. Some farmers object to this policy fearing it will

New housing in Lalibela

increase disease and interfere with agriculture. The government reasons that living in villages will improve health facilities, education, electrification, and marketing. Some outside observers think moving the farmers to villages will make it easier for the government to control them.

In Addis Ababa and the other cities, the people are organized into small groups called *kebelles*. The kebelles are designed to help the city dwellers in much the same way the peasant associations help the farm families.

The peasant associations and kebelles are not free to do as they please, though. They are expected to implement the policies of Mengistu's central government, but they are responsible for organizing communal labor on public projects and carrying out government policies. In the future they may be able to assist in providing schools, public health facilities, and an overall improvement in production.

Addis Ababa is the hub of Ethiopia.

Addis Ababa

Chapter 7

THE CITIES OF ETHIOPIA

ADDIS ABABA, ETHIOPIA'S CAPITAL

The capital city of Addis Ababa, with 1.5 million people, is by far the largest of Ethiopia's few cities. In fact, more people live in Addis Ababa than inhabit Ethiopia's ten next most populous cities combined!

Addis Ababa is an interesting blend of old and new. Thousands of the city's poorer people live in mud houses similar to the ones in which rural Ethiopians live. Not far from the mud houses, dozens of new structures, mostly built since 1960, give parts of Addis Ababa a very modern look. Among these new buildings are hotels and movie theaters, high-rise offices and residences, night clubs, and a few mansions.

Located almost at Ethiopia's exact center, Addis Ababa is the country's hub in almost every way. As the country's capital, it is the meeting place for its national lawmakers. The national government is still housed in a palace built by Menilek II.

Addis Ababa is also the manufacturing, transportation, and educational center. A large percentage of the country's factories

The Lion of Judah Monument (left)
and the market (right) in Addis Ababa

are located in the city. Among the goods produced are textiles, cement, sugar, tobacco, shoes, foods, plastics, and chemicals.

When people or products come to Ethiopia, they usually arrive in Addis Ababa first, and when people or products leave the country, they usually leave via the capital city. Addis Ababa is the site of the country's main airport. Ethiopia's main railroad connects Addis Ababa to the city of Djibouti in the country of Djibouti to the east on the Gulf of Aden. And Addis Ababa is connected to the country's other main cities by a growing system of highways.

Because Addis Ababa is Ethiopia's commercial center, its people have a higher income than people in other regions. As a result, people from other areas of the country have poured into Addis Ababa in recent years, swelling the city's population from 800,000 in 1971 to nearly twice that many in 1987. Many of the newcomers cannot find work, though, because there are not enough jobs for Addis Ababa's fast-growing population. Urban unemployment is one of Ethiopia's most serious problems.

*Above: City Hall, one of the new buildings erected in Addis Ababa since 1960.
Below: A procession celebrating* Maskal, *a Christian holy day (left) and a typical
street scene in one of the older parts of Addis Ababa (right)*

Colorful basketry items (above left) and butter (above right) for sale in
the market in Addis Ababa. Below: An unusual building on a street corner

The Bank of Ethiopia (left) and Africa Hall (right)

Besides having a higher average income, Addis Ababans have a much higher average educational level than other Ethiopians. The city has a higher ratio of schools than other areas of the country, and the capital is also the site of Ethiopia's most important university. Until the revolution it was called Haile Sellassie I University, but since 1975 its name has been Addis Ababa University. The university has several branches in the country and schools of medicine, education, science, and graduate studies.

The capital city is Ethiopia's cultural and communication center, too. Addis Ababa is home to most of the major museums and libraries. And most of the country's radio and TV broadcasting and publishing are done here.

The United Nations Economic Commission for Africa meets in a lovely building called Africa Hall. The Organization of African Unity (OAU), a fifty-nation group that works to improve life for Africans, also meets in Africa Hall. Because of these important meetings of African leaders that have been held in Addis Ababa in recent years, the city has been called "the capital of Africa."

The Massawa road and railway, both leading to Asmara

ASMARA, ETHIOPIA'S SECOND-LARGEST CITY

With a population of about half a million people, Asmara, located about five hundred miles (eight hundred kilometers) north of Addis Ababa in the province of Eritrea, is Ethiopia's second-largest city. Until the 1880s, Asmara was just a little village. Its growth began when Ras Alula, a famous Ethiopian army commander, made it his headquarters.

Several thousand Italians still live in Asmara, and the Italian influence can be seen in the city. Sections of Asmara have villas, sidewalk cafes, and tree-lined streets that resemble those in Italy. Asmara also has large neighborhoods where thousands of poor people live, crowded together in small stone houses.

Asmara is home to the University of Asmara. Ethiopia's second major airport is here, and the city is a manufacturing center where textiles, shoes, and soft drinks are made.

About half of Asmara's people are Muslims, while the other half are Christians. Among the city's most interesting landmarks are the Grand Mosque, where Muslims worship, and several large Christian churches.

Above: Asmara is Ethiopia's second-largest city. Left: The Grand Mosque in Asmara

Marketplace (above) and colorful pastel buildings (left) in Dire Dawa

DIRE DAWA

Ethiopia's third-biggest city, Dire Dawa, has about 100,000 people. It is located in a hot, dry region about 200 miles (322 kilometers) east of Addis Ababa. The town grew during the early 1900s, when the railroad linking Addis Ababa with Djibouti passed through. The town shows the influence of the railroad to the region. The population is a mix of Muslim Somali, Issa, Afar, and Christian Amhara.

Today coffee and meats are produced in Dire Dawa, and cloth and cement are made here. Dire Dawa is in the heart of eastern Ethiopia, which is mainly Muslim. Two of the town's best-known features are a very old mosque and an old Muslim cemetery.

A busy market (left) and a shop in front of a small mosque (right) in Harar

HARAR

Just 35 miles (56 kilometers) southeast of Dire Dawa is Harar, a city of sixty thousand people, one of Ethiopia's main Islamic centers. One of the country's oldest cities, Harar was settled by Muslims from Arabia in the seventh century. For centuries the Muslims and the Christians in the area fought each other. It was from Harar that Ahmed Gran began his holy war against the Christians in the 1520s. After Ahmed Gran's death in 1543, the Muslims built a five-gated wall around Harar to protect the city from the Christians. That 450-year-old wall is still standing.

One of Harar's most famous buildings is the old Muslim mosque with its twin minarets. Five times a day muezzins climb the minarets to call the city's Muslims to prayer. Harar also has a

Above: The Blue Nile (left) and children with handwoven umbrellas (right) near Bahar Dar   Below: Gondar, located north of Lake Tana

famous *megallah*, or outdoor Muslim marketplace, as well as a separate Christian marketplace. Harar's Muslims and Christians for the most part cooperate today and work at producing coffee, basketry, and jewelry.

In both Harar and Dire Dawa a narcotic leaf called *chat* is traded. Chat is one of Ethiopia's major exports to the Red Sea trade. Although the Ethiopian government discourages the cultivating and use of chat, it is legal in many countries in the Red Sea area. Somalia, however, has outlawed its use and importation.

BAHAR DAR

Probably the fastest-growing city in Ethiopia is Bahar Dar, located on the banks of Lake Tana near the source of the Blue Nile. Nearby are the Blue Nile Falls and a hydroelectric dam that provides power for the city and a large textile factory. Bahar Dar Polytechnic is located here.

GONDAR

Located north of Lake Tana in northwestern Ethiopia, Gondar was just a tiny village until Emperor Fasilidas made it his capital in 1632. During the more than two centuries that Gondar served as Ethiopia's capital, several castles and over forty churches were built in the city. These are now among the most interesting historical buildings in the entire country.

Although it was home to eighty thousand people at its height, Gondar's population dropped after Emperor Tewodros chose Mekdela as his main capital during the 1850s. The population

Above: A view of the city of Gondar from the imperial compound
Below: Dese, a market town

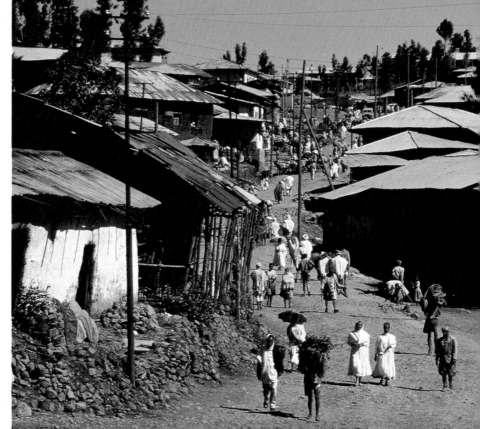

climbed again during the twentieth century especially with the Italian occupation.

Besides a large number of Christians, Gondar is home to many Muslims and a small number of Ethiopian Jews, the Falashas. Most of the people in the Gondar area are farmers. Gondar is also the site of the Public Health College, which is part of Addis Ababa University.

DESE

Also spelled Dessie or Dessye, Dese is a town of seventy thousand people located about 200 miles (322 kilometers) northeast of Addis Ababa. Dese is a market town where trade from the Denakil Depression and the highlands meet. Afar people with their camels and goats trade with highland Oromo and Amhara to obtain grain, cloth, and manufactured goods, from highland markets. Mekdela, where Emperor Tewodros made his last stand over a century ago, is not far from Dese.

JIMA

The province of Kefa, a great coffee-growing area, is in the southwest. Jima, the biggest city in the province with its sixty thousand people, is an important center for gathering coffee that is grown in the region.

Jima is also famed for its wood carvers. The well-known "Jima stools" and many wooden musical instruments are made in the town.

Above: Farmers winnowing wheat   Below: A woman grinding red peppers (left) and livestock at a desert watering hole (right)

Chapter 8

THE WORK
OF ETHIOPIANS

AGRICULTURE

The most important food crops grown in Ethiopia are grains—
teff (a grain grown only in Ethiopia), wheat, barley, corn,
sorghum, and millet. Small farmers also grow a variety of peas
and beans, including chick-peas, field peas, and lentils. Other food
crops grown by Ethiopians include peppers and other spices,
sweet potatoes, onions, squash, and oil seeds, such as sesame,
safflower, and peanuts.

Many Ethiopian farm families also raise livestock. In fact,
Ethiopia has the most livestock of any African nation—about 100
million animals, or nearly three times the country's human
population. Cattle, sheep, and goats are the most common
livestock animals. Although some cattle are raised for meat or
milk, most pull plows and do other farm work. Most of Ethiopia's
cattle are the humped kind known as zebus. The sheep provide
meat and skins for the farm families, and the goats are raised
mainly for meat, but in some areas for milk. Donkeys, mules,
horses, and camels also are used as beasts of burden and for
transportation, and some people drink the rich camel's milk.

Left: Salt workers brewing coffee   Right: A weaver working at his loom

To the rest of the world, coffee is Ethiopia's best-known crop. According to one story, hundreds of years ago some Ethiopian goatherds noticed that their animals did not get sleepy at night after eating the beans on the coffee trees. This reputedly gave people the idea of making a stimulating drink out of the coffee beans. This drink was named coffee, perhaps after Ethiopia's southwestern province of Kefa.

Today Kefa is still a great coffee-growing area, as are several other regions of the country. Ethiopia as a whole is about the sixth leading coffee-producing country in the world. Some of the coffee is grown on large government-run plantations, but much of the crop grows both cultivated and wild on small-holders' land.

Little of the coffee is packaged in Ethiopia. Most of it is exported to the United States, the Soviet Union, and other countries, where it is processed and packaged. Coffee beans are Ethiopia's most important export crop. Other farm products that are exported to

A sesame oil mill (left) and workers prying a salt slab loose (right) at a salt lake in the Denakil Depression

other nations include animal hides and skins, chat, oilseeds, vegetables, and frozen meats. Many farmers also grow cotton that is used in Ethiopia's textile industry.

MANUFACTURING

As late as the early 1900s, there was almost no manufacturing in Ethiopia. Only in the last few years has there been a sizable amount of industry in the country. About ten percent of Ethiopians work at making industrial products today. Most of the country's manufacturing is done in its two major cities—Addis Ababa and Asmara—but some products are made in several of the other larger cities.

The making of textiles is one of Ethiopia's most important industries. Foods and beverages made from farm goods are other major products. Chemicals, wood and plastic products, cement

Left: A young nomad herding goats on a dry riverbed   Right: At an irrigation canal near Tendaho, people fill containers with water to sell in town.

and bricks, shoes, and steel also are made in Ethiopia. The United States is a major trade partner, but Japan, Italy, the Soviet Union, and East Germany are among the main buyers of Ethiopian products.

AGRICULTURE AND MANUFACTURING MUST IMPROVE

As of the mid-1980s, Ethiopia was the world's sixth-poorest nation. Its people had one of the shortest average life spans, lowest average incomes, lowest literacy rates, and highest rates of infant death.

To solve these problems, Ethiopia desperately needs to improve its agricultural and manufacturing output. Ethiopian farmers must learn modern farming techniques and obtain modern tools so that they can produce more food. The country must enlarge its industries so that there will be more jobs and money for its people.

A Christian Orthodox priest (left) and a soldier (right)

The government has tried to improve Ethiopia's manufacturing and farming. But some people feel that the government has not done enough in these areas.

OTHER WAYS OF MAKING A LIVING

About ten of every hundred Ethiopians work outside the fields of agriculture and manufacturing. Several hundred thousand serve as priests and holy men in the country's many thousands of churches and mosques. Over three hundred thousand serve in Ethiopia's armed forces, which are among the largest in all of Africa.

The government employs many thousands of Ethiopians, ranging from teachers and bankers to coffee pickers and street cleaners. The numbers of Ethiopians working for the government has increased dramatically since the revolution. The government also owns the national airline—Ethiopian Airlines.

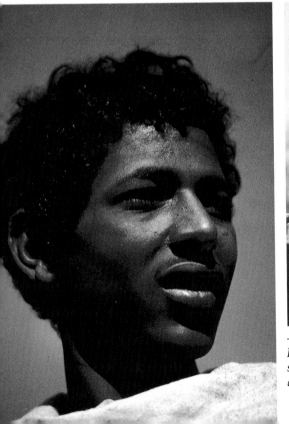

Faces of Ethiopia, clockwise from top left: A Tigray
salt miner, Tigrayan shepherds, Amhara girls,
and a young Amhara man

Chapter 9

THE PEOPLE AND
THEIR CULTURE

PEOPLES AND LANGUAGES

One historian has called Ethiopia a "museum of peoples." Very few countries have as great a variety of people and life-styles. Although some are rather small, there are at least seventy separate ethnic groups speaking at least seventy separate languages in Ethiopia. One reason for Ethiopia's diversity is its closeness to Asia and Europe.

The Oromo people live mainly in the southern half of the country and are Ethiopia's largest group. The Oromos comprise as much as 40 percent of the population. Most of them are Muslims, but some are Christians and others worship their own traditional god. Their language is called Afan Oromo.

About a third of the population are Amhara and Tigray people, who for so long were the country's dominant groups. Both groups are Christian, but some Muslims live among them sharing their language. Amharic and Tigrinya, their languages, are related to both Hebrew and Arabic. The ancient language of Ge'ez was also related as a member of the Semitic language family. Although no longer spoken in daily life, Ge'ez is used in church services and in scholarly writings.

There are about a million Somali people in Ethiopia, mostly in the eastern part of the country. A Muslim people, the Somalis speak the Somali language, and some also speak Arabic.

HOUSING

Ethiopians live in a variety of housing, including small circular one-room houses, stone houses, apartment buildings, and luxurious villas. Every ethnic group of Ethiopia has a different style of house. Out in the country a common type of dwelling is the one-room round house, called a *gocho*. To build their gocho, the Ethiopian family first makes walls out of strong, thin saplings. Often these wooden walls are covered by a plaster made of straw and clay. The beehive-shaped roof is made of wood covered with grass. Rectangular houses have tin roofs that are helpful in collecting water during the rains.

In the countryside, parents and children live inside the crowded and smoky houses. Some families also keep their chickens and other smaller animals in a section of the house at night so that they will be safe from hyenas and wild dogs.

Most of the rural dwellers sleep on animal skins or wooden beds. The cooking is done in a fireplace usually built in the middle of the house. There is no chimney, but most of the smoke escapes through the top of the roof. Clothes and tools are hung from pegs on the walls. Few rural Ethiopians have much furniture other than the three-legged stools that are so common in Ethiopia and a portable table woven out of straw called a *masob*.

Those Ethiopians who move about with their herds take their homes, often portable huts made of tree branches and overlaid with grass mats, with them. The nomads can take these movable

Nomads in front of their portable home (left), which can be easily packed up and moved on the back of a camel (right)

homes off the backs of their camels and assemble them in a short while. Cooking is usually done outside these portable houses.

Especially in the northern part of the country, some Ethiopians live in stone buildings. Some of these homes are rectangular, but others are round and are as high as two stories.

DRESS

A wide variety of clothing can be seen in Ethiopia, ranging from loincloths to the latest fashions. A common garment worn by the Amharic and Tigrayan men and women is the *shamma*, a rectangular shawl about 5 by 10 feet (1.5 by 3 meters). The shamma is draped over the shoulders and arms and sometimes over the head. Women often wear their shammas over a white cotton gown called *k'amis*. Many men wear a shirt and white trousers under their shammas.

Left: Many Oromo women wear colorful jewelry.
Right: Drying maize

In recent years increasing numbers of Ethiopians, especially city dwellers, have changed to a Western style of dress. But the people who wear business suits to work may wear traditional clothes at home or with their friends.

Most Ethiopians love to wear jewelry. Earrings, bracelets, colorful bead necklaces, and crosses and other religious emblems are commonly seen throughout the country. Oromo women in the east wear beautiful amber necklaces. Many Tigrayan women wear gold earrings and necklaces. Many men, especially those from rural villages, carry a *dula*, or walking stick. The dula helps the man pick his way over rough terrain. It also can be used as a prop when he stops to chat with a neighbor or can even be turned into a deadly weapon.

FOOD

For millions of Ethiopians, getting enough food is the number-one problem. Since the days of Solomon and Sheba, many

Tigrayan nomads wrap dough around hot stones and bake bread in ashes (left). Barley is roasted (right) to make beer, called talla.

Ethiopians have died because of a lack of food. But when they do have enough food, Ethiopians enjoy a tasty and nutritious diet.

A staple in Ethiopia is a sourdough pancake-bread called *injera*. Usually made out of teff, injera is eaten by many Ethiopians at almost every meal. Sometimes injera is also made of wheat, barley, sorghum, or even corn.

Also popular is a spicy stew dish called *wat* that is made with vegetables, and on special occasions chucks of chicken or beef are added. Injera and wat are eaten together. Pieces of the injera are broken off and used to scoop up the wat.

Both adults and children enjoy a home-brewed beer called *talla*, which is made from barley. Talla is only mildly alcoholic, but *tej*, a wine made from honey, is much stronger. Milk (from cows, camels, and goats), coffee, and herb teas are other popular drinks. Ethiopians have special ceremonies for preparing and drinking coffee.

A Falasha man and his child (left) and priests dancing at a Christian religious celebration (right)

RELIGION

The latest census says that Ethiopia's population is forty-two million. The population is growing at 2.8 percent per year. It is estimated that about 40 percent are Christians and about 40 percent are Muslims. Several million Ethiopians are neither Christians nor Muslims, but follow various traditional religions in which they worship their own god. Ethiopia also has a few thousand Jewish people, the Falashas, who live mainly in the Gondar region in the northwest.

The Falashas place six-pointed Stars of David over the buildings that serve as their synagogues, and also follow many other Jewish traditions. Where did these Ethiopian Jews come from, and how did they get to Ethiopia? The Falashas say that they were a "lost tribe" of Israel that broke away from the main group when Moses led the Jews out of Egypt over three thousand years ago. However, some scholars think that the Falashas were converted to Judaism

Christian priests carry Arks of the Covenant, covered in brocades, on their heads in a procession commemorating the Epiphany.

at a later date—but still before the birth of Christ. Either way, the Falashas have lived near Lake Tana for over two thousand years. Until the 1860s, when they became known to the outside world, the Falashas thought they were the only Jews on earth!

There are similarities in the religious practices of Ethiopia's Christians, Muslims, and Jews. Although Christians in other parts of the world eat pork, the Ethiopian Orthodox church forbids the eating of pork. The Jews and the Muslims are forbidden to eat pork also. All three religions have special fast days.

The holy books and basic teachings of the three religions are also similar. Parts of the Muslims' holy book, the Koran, contain stories about figures that appear in the Old (Jewish) and New (Christian) Testaments. The Ethiopian Christians use a great deal of Old Testament material in their practices and beliefs. For example, the emperors were said to have been descendants of the biblical King Solomon. Haile Sellassie was often called the ''Lion of Judah,'' the symbol of Ethiopia's Solomonic dynasty.

There are even similarities in how the three groups celebrate various holidays. Among the Christians' holy days are *Faskia* (Easter), *Genna* (Christmas), *Maskal* (celebrating the finding of the cross used to crucify Jesus), and *Timkat* (celebrating Jesus' baptism).

Among the Falashas' important holidays are Passover (a festival commemorating the freeing of the Jews from Egyptian slavery) and the Day of Atonement (a day when Jews ask God to forgive them for their sins). A very sacred time for the Muslims is the ninth month of their year, *Ramadan,* when they are supposed to fast between dawn and sunset.

Until the revolution, Christianity was considered Ethiopia's official religion, despite the fact that millions of people who followed other religions lived in the country. One of the fairest acts of the government has been to proclaim all religions equal in the eyes of the law.

FAMILY LIFE

Ethiopian families tend to be large, with the work strictly divided among the mothers, fathers, and children. Parents have large families because they fear famine and disease will claim the lives of some of their children. Work is assigned according to age and sex, because that is an easy way for each generation to learn what is expected of them. Unlike some other African families, Ethiopians are nuclear, not transgenerational families. This means they are made up of a mother, father, and children and sometimes a relative or two.

The father is expected to do the farm work—planting the seeds, weeding the fields, and harvesting the crops. Since most Ethiopian

Left: A pair of oxen and a traditional plow
Right: A young girl carrying water from a well

farmers depend on ox-pulled wooden plows and few have modern tools, this is extremely hard work. Traditionally the men are the heads of the families and their word is considered law, but the government is working to promote equality among the sexes.

The mothers work just as hard. In the fields they weed and sometimes help harvest. They cook the injera and wat, brew the talla, and prepare everything else the family eats and drinks. They also do the housework, as well as most of the child raising.

At age five or younger, children start helping with the work. Young children gather kindling for the fire and feed the chickens. Later they learn to stand watch in the fields to keep the baboons and birds away from the crops. Older boys herd the livestock and help their fathers with the farm work, while older girls help their mothers cook and care for the younger children.

Childhood is a very serious time for most Ethiopian boys and girls. Few have toys, and less than half go to school. For many children, their happiest times are the religious holidays when they

A parade of schoolchildren in Adami Tulu

enjoy special feasts, dances, music, and games. By their late teens, most young people are starting families of their own.

There are a number of marriage customs among the various people of Ethiopia. But generally Ethiopian women marry young—usually by age fifteen. The young men usually wed at a slightly older age—the late teens or early twenties. In most cases one man marries one woman, but some groups allow a man to marry more than one woman simultaneously. Divorces are commonplace.

The newlyweds often live for a while in a house built on the property of the groom's parents. After several months or even a year, the couple move into their own house, and then begin to raise their family.

Among some city people, these traditional roles of men, women, and children have changed. In the cities some women work outside the home as teachers, clerks, or even taxi drivers, and some children live much like young people in more developed countries.

Children from the Lake Tana region

EDUCATION

Ethiopia's rugged terrain has helped keep outsiders from conquering the country, but it has hindered other kinds of progress. About 75 percent of all Ethiopians live farther than half a day's walk from a good road. Many children cannot get an education because there are no roads leading to the nearest school. A poor transportation system is a prime reason why so few of Ethiopia's children attend school.

For the fortunate young people who do attend school, there are four levels of education. First comes elementary school, where they learn such basics as reading and writing. Then comes junior high, high school, and college. Few Ethiopians finish high school, and very, very few attend college.

Since the revolution, some children have been taught in their native languages, not just in Amharic as was once the case. Students begin studying English in third grade and by seventh

A scroll of the Ethiopian Bible

grade most subjects are taught in English. The government is continually building new schools, including ones where adults are taught to read and write.

LITERATURE, MUSIC, AND ART

Ethiopia has had a rich literary tradition for many centuries. Most of Ethiopia's early books related to Christianity or history, and were written and read by men who were educated in the country's monasteries and religious schools.

One important old Christian literary work is the *Kebra Negast* (*Glory of Kings*). First written in about the 1300s, the *Kebra Negast* enlarges upon the biblical Solomon and Sheba story, and recounts how later emperors were descended from the biblical pair. Another important book, *Fetha Negast* (*Law of Kings*) dates back to perhaps the 1100s, and compiles the laws of the medieval rulers. It influences the Ethiopian legal system even today.

Among the early religious books was *The Book of the Mysteries of Heaven and Earth*, which dates from the late 1300s. This book describes a number of religious topics, including a battle between Satan and the archangel Michael. *Life and Acts*, dating from about the 1400s, tells about the Ethiopian saint, Tekla Haymanot.

Oral tradition is especially strong in the south, west, and southeast, where many societies have rich oral poetry and narratives of their kings and of their past. Somalis are known especially for the ability to memorize oral poetry word for word and retain it for many years.

The Amharic and Tigrayan languages also have a unique literary form, a kind of poetry called *sam-enna-warq*, meaning "wax and gold." The name comes from the Ethiopian goldsmith's technique of pouring liquid gold into a mold made with wax and clay. Although he starts with something as simple and valueless as wax, the craftsman eventually produces a golden object. In the same vein, the wax meaning of the poem is simple and not very interesting. But, due to a play on words, there is a second more fascinating and complex meaning to the poem—the "gold."

Developed by the Amhara hundreds of years ago, wax and gold poems are still composed by Ethiopians on many subjects, including politics, religion, and romance. The following excerpt demonstrates the form:

Yamin tiqem talla yamin tiqem tajji?
Tallat sishanu buna adargaw enji.

Talla is the Ethiopian barley beer, while *tajji* is a poetic way of saying tej, the Ethiopian honey wine. Translated, the wax meaning of the poem is:

A priest in Lalibela beats a drum to announce that the Arks of the Covenant are being taken out of the churches in celebration of the Epiphany.

> Of what use is talla, of what use is tej?
>
> When seeing an enemy off, serve him coffee.

In other words, don't waste liquor on your enemies. However, when the words *"buna adargaw,"* meaning "serve him coffee," are said quickly, they become *"bun adargaw,"* meaning "reduce him to ashes." The gold meaning of the poem is:

> Of what use is talla, of what use is tej?
>
> When seeing an enemy off, reduce him to ashes.

People who were afraid to come out with their remarks directly hid the criticism in the wax and gold poems.

In the twentieth century, several Ethiopian authors have written novels. One of the most popular novelists is a man named Sahle Sellassie, author of *Shinega's Village: Scenes of Ethiopian Life*, *Firebrands*, and *Warrior King*.

Ethiopia also has an ancient musical tradition. Many of the songs and dances performed in the Ethiopian church date from the 500s. During religious dances, an ancient drum called a *kaboro* is beaten while a rattle called a *tsenatsel* is shaken.

Two Ethiopian musical instruments; a washint *(left) and a* krar *(right)*

Out in the fields, the shepherds sometimes play a wooden flute called a *washint*. According to an old shepherds' belief, the bubbling sounds from the washint calm the animals. Two other Ethiopian musical instruments are a kind of harp called a *begenna* and a banjo called a *krar*.

For centuries, Ethiopia has been home to the *azmaris*, musicians who roam the countryside singing ballads and folk songs much like the European minstrels of the Middle Ages. The azmaris play a one-stringed fiddle called a *masinko* while singing about such topics as love, war, and politics.

Like the wax and gold poetry, the azmaris's songs about political figures often had a double meaning. During the Italian occupation at the start of World War II, the azmaris traveled from place to place singing of how the emperor would one day return and defeat the *ferenji* (foreigners). Although their numbers have dwindled, there are still some azmaris in Ethiopia.

Nearly all of the best architecture, painting, and carving has been religious in nature. People from around the world visit

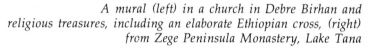
A mural (left) in a church in Debre Birhan and
religious treasures, including an elaborate Ethiopian cross, (right)
from Zege Peninsula Monastery, Lake Tana

Ethiopia to see its impressive old churches and castles. The biblical
scenes painted on the walls and ceilings of some churches are
divided into many separate pictures which, if viewed one after the
other, tell a story.

Craftsmen have long been famous for producing a special kind
of cross, called a *maskal* or Ethiopian cross, out of metal or wood.
Many Christian Ethiopians wear simple versions of this cross.
More elaborate Ethiopian crosses are carried in religious
processions. Other people produce beautiful cloth and jewelry in
silver and gold.

A number of modern Ethiopians have become internationally
famous in the art world. One of the best-known Ethiopian artists
is Afewerk Tekle. His beautiful stained-glass windows can be
viewed in Africa Hall in Addis Ababa.

GAMES AND SPORTS

When the Italians seized control of Ethiopia during the 1930s,
they introduced soccer to the country. Since then soccer has

Stained-glass windows by Afewerk Tekle in Africa Hall

become very popular. There are dozens of soccer clubs in Addis Ababa, and teams also play in many other parts of the country. Each province sends its best team to the national championship tournament, held at the stadium at Addis Ababa University.

Basketball, volleyball, and bicycle racing are popular also, especially among the students, in Addis Ababa and the other cities.

Out in the country, several special games are played on holidays. During the Genna season, many Ethiopians play a game called *genna*, which resembles field hockey. Opposing teams try to knock a leather, or wooden, ball across each other's goal.

Ethiopia has produced a number of world-famous athletes, especially in track. Three times in a row—in 1960, 1964, and 1968—Ethiopian runners won the gold medal for the marathon race in the Olympic Games. The first two times the gold was taken by Abebe Bikila, while in 1968 the gold was brought home to Ethiopia by Mamo Wolde. In 1980 the Ethiopian runner Miruts Yifter claimed the gold medal for the Olympic 5,000-meter and 10,000-meter races.

Traditional values and beliefs are passed from the
old to the young by example and by folktales,
which usually have a moral.

Chapter 10

ETHIOPIAN FOLKTALES

Even though few of them could read or write, Ethiopians of all languages and religions of past centuries found a way to teach their values and beliefs to their young. They did it by telling them stories. The Ethiopians were, and still are, among the world's greatest storytellers.

The characters in the stories are often poor people or animals with human traits—the hungry leopard, lordly lion, clever baboon or monkey, wise elephant, and persecuted snake. The qualities promoted in the stories are faithfulness, kindness, and cleverness. In many stories, a small person or animal beats a larger one through brains, not brawn, and poor people are rewarded for their acts of kindness.

THE SNAKE WHO HELPED THE MAN

(A story of the Gurage, a people who live mainly in and near Addis Ababa)

Four creatures—a rat, a man, a monkey, and a snake—were on the road heading to a distant land when the sun set. They stopped at the house of a wealthy merchant and asked if they could spend the night there.

"All of you are welcome except the snake," said the merchant, "because snakes cannot be trusted."

"You let the man in, and he is the cruelest creature on the earth," cried the snake, who was quite insulted.

The merchant felt sorry for the snake and let him sleep inside with the other three. They were all very polite guests, and the merchant was a perfect host. In the morning the four thanked the man and continued on their way.

During the next few years the merchant's luck changed and he lost his fortune. When he reached the point where he had to beg for injera to eat, he remembered the four creatures he had helped long ago.

The merchant first tracked down the rat, who felt so sorry for him that she gave him some gold coins. When he found the man next, the merchant thought he was in luck. If the lowly rat had given him gold, what might the man give him? But the man stole the gold coins, then pushed the merchant into a deep ditch by the side of the road and left him there.

The merchant was lying there expecting to die of hunger, when suddenly the monkey came by and saw him. The monkey reached down and helped pull the man out of the ditch.

Once the monkey was gone, the merchant took stock of his situation. He was worse off than before he had gone looking for his four old guests, because now he was cold and wet in addition to poor. He was standing there feeling sorry for himself when the snake came slithering through the grass by the side of the road. "What happened to you?" inquired the snake.

After the merchant told him everything, the snake said, "Didn't I tell you that man is the cruelest creature on earth? I will help you. Come with me."

The merchant and the snake went to the estate of the region's richest landowner. The snake waited until the landowner's daughter stepped outside. As the merchant admired her beauty, the snake slithered up and bit the young lady.

"Why did you do that?" the merchant asked, when his friend returned.

"Just wait, and do everything I say," answered the snake.

The girl was brought inside the house and a doctor was called in, but she became very ill. Meanwhile, the snake went into the forest and brewed up a special snakebite medicine. "Take this and knock on the door," said the snake. "And here is what you are to do..."

Just when it seemed certain that the young lady would die, the merchant knocked on the door. He promised to save the rich landowner's daughter, if he could have her hand in marriage.

"Anything, but please save her!" answered the father.

The merchant went to the beautiful young lady's room. He gave the girl the snake's special medicine, and suddenly she opened her eyes and sat up in bed. The girl's father kept his word and arranged for a splendid wedding. As far as is known, the couple enjoyed a healthy, wealthy, and long life.

A GIFT OF AN ORANGE

(A story of the Falashas)

One morning when a farmer went out to his field, he found an orange so perfect that he was certain it was a gift from heaven. The poor farmer showed the orange to his wife and children and to the other farmers in the village. They all agreed that an orange

103

so beautiful and perfectly shaped had to be a gift from God.

The farmer offered the orange to one member of his family after another, but they all said that the orange was meant for a king. That gave the farmer an idea. He would take the orange to the king and give it to him.

His wife wrapped a fine cloth around the orange, and the farmer began walking toward the capital. When he reached the palace, the farmer opened the cloth, so that the guards could see the orange shining like the sun. A few minutes later they returned with the king.

The farmer explained how he had found the orange, and how everyone thought it was a gift from God. "I want you to have it," the man said.

"Such a gift deserves a gift in return," the king said, turning the orange in his hands. "What can I give you?"

"It is enough that you are pleased," the man answered. He then left the palace and started walking home.

The king was so touched by the man's generosity that he sent several servants out with his favorite horse. The servants caught up with the farmer and insisted that he accept the horse as a gift. The happy farmer then rode home on the horse that had belonged to his king.

The story of the simple farmer who had been given a fine horse in exchange for an orange circulated through the capital city. It gave a greedy merchant an idea. "If a farmer received a horse for an orange, what might I get if I give the king a horse?" thought the man. Dreaming of riches, he took his best horse out of his stable and brought it to the king.

"I know you gave your best horse to a farmer," said the merchant, "so I now give you my best horse."

Waterfowl, including white pelicans, at the Lake Abaya Game Preserve

"Thank you," said the king, but he could tell by the man's attitude that he expected something better in return. "Such a gift deserves a special gift in return," the king added. "Wait here."

When he returned, the king handed the merchant a cloth. The man eagerly unwrapped it, but was crestfallen when he saw that only an orange was inside. The merchant was too greedy to realize what a perfect orange it was.

"This orange was given me by a man with a good heart," said the king. "I give it to you in the hope that it will give you a better heart than the one you have."

SOME OUTSTANDING ETHIOPIANS

TEWODROS II

Kassa, the son of a local chieftain, was born near Lake Tana in northwestern Ethiopia in about 1818. After Kassa's father died, the boy and his mother were so poor that she had to sell *kosso*, a drug used against tapeworm, in the streets of Gondar. When Kassa was about nine years old, he went to study at a monastery near Lake Tana where he became a devout Christian. He was a fine scholar, and by twenty he knew a great deal about the Bible, history, and law. He was also a surprisingly fierce warrior who fought at the side of his older half-brother.

After his half-brother died, Kassa became a *shifta* (bandit) who specialized in holding up Muslim caravans transporting goods to Egypt. More and more men joined his band, and soon Kassa was one of western Ethiopia's most powerful leaders. "The kosso vendor's son," as his enemies called him, seized one province after another. Finally, in early 1855, he became emperor.

There was an old Ethiopian prophecy that one day an emperor named Tewodros (or Theodore) would usher in an era of "happiness, plenty, and peace" that would last for a thousand years. Kassa adopted Tewodros II as his crown name because he felt he was destined to fulfill that prophecy.

Unlike most previous emperors, Tewodros sought contact with Europeans because he thought they could help him modernize Ethiopia. He hired a number of Germans to help make cannons, and he also had several Englishmen at his court.

During his early years as emperor, Tewodros worked to improve his country. However, several events in his personal life apparently helped bring him down. During an 1860 uprising, rebels killed Walter Plowden, an English diplomat who had become friendly with Tewodros. That same year during a revenge-seeking expedition, John Bell, an Englishman whom Tewodros considered a brother, was shot to death while trying to protect the emperor. At about the same time, Tewodros's first wife died. After these three deaths, Tewodros began drinking a great deal of alcohol. He also became a tyrant who tortured and killed thousands of his enemies.

One of the strangest events in Ethiopian history resulted in Tewodros's downfall. The emperor hoped that Great Britain might help him drive the Muslims out of Egypt, Jerusalem, and the rest of the Holy Land. But he had a misunderstanding with the British and he became angry. He captured some English officials who were in his country and threw them into prison

at Amba Mekdala. When the British sent a diplomat to obtain the release of the prisoners, Tewodros threw him and some other Europeans into prison, too.

The British decided to rescue their people from the Amba Mekdala fortress. In early 1868 a British force consisting of several thousand men under Robert Napier arrived at the northern coast of Ethiopia along the Red Sea. The British loaded their supplies onto their thousands of camels and mules, and their cannons onto their forty-four elephants. The ground was so mountainous that it took the Napier expedition three months to travel the 400 miles (644 kilometers) to Tewodros's stronghold.

By this time Tewodros was so hated by his people that no kings came to help him. As the British approached, Tewodros released the Europeans from the Amba Mekdala prison. "I chained you," he told them, "because people believed that I was not a strong king. Now that your masters are coming, I release you to show that I am not afraid."

The next day Tewodros told his people, "You hear of white men coming to fight me. It is no rumor." When one of his soldiers shouted that they would beat the British, Tewodros answered, "You fool, you do not know what you say! These people have long cannons, elephants, guns, and muskets without number. We cannot fight against them!"

Tewodros's words proved true. On April 10, 1868, the emperor's forces were badly beaten by the British in a battle near Amba Mekdala. The main body of British troops was not even involved in this battle, which was won by the expedition's advance guard. Then, as the British marched still closer to Amba Mekdala, an assistant urged Tewodros to kill the European ex-prisoners who were waiting for the soldiers to come and take them away. "You donkey!" Tewodros answered, "Have I not killed enough these last two days? Do you want me to kill these white men and cover Abyssinia with blood?"

Realizing that it was a matter of hours before the British would arrive, Tewodros went into his tent and dictated a final statement to his secretary:

> Out of what I have done of evil towards my people, may God bring good. His will be done. I had intended, if God had so decreed, to conquer the whole world; and it was my desire to die if my purpose could not be fulfilled. Since the day of my birth till now no man has dared to lay hands on me. Whenever my soldiers began to waver in battle, it was mine to arise and rally them. Last night the darkness hindered me from doing so. You people who have passed the night

in joy [those who were glad for Tewodros's defeat], may God do unto you as He has done unto me. I had hoped, after subduing all my enemies in Abyssinia, to lead my army against Jerusalem.

The next day, April 13, 1868, British troops used ladders to storm Amba Mekdala. Tewodros gave his soldiers permission to run for their lives, and all but one hundred fled down the steep paths to the ground below. Tewodros did not allow any man to "lay hands" on him, as he had said the day before. Just before the enemy reached him, Tewodros committed suicide.

When Napier left Ethiopia he took the dead emperor's wife and six-year-old son with him. The queen died en route, but the son arrived in England where he attended Oxford University, but he died at age eighteen.

MENILEK II

Sahle Mariam was born in the town of Ankober, about 100 miles (160 kilometers) northeast of present-day Abbis Ababa, in 1844. His father was king of Shewa, which now is a province but then was a powerful kingdom within Ethiopia.

In 1855, when Sahle was eleven years old, Emperor Tewodros easily conquered Shewa; Sahle's father died of illness; and, to insure that Sahle would never lead a rebellion against him, Tewodros imprisoned the boy at his fortress on Amba Mekdala.

Tewodros treated Sahle Mariam kindly. He saw to the boy's education and allowed him to meet the many Europeans who came to his court. When Sahle Mariam was sixteen years old, the emperor gave his own daughter to the young man in marriage. Tewodros thought that he could exchange his daughter for Sahle Mariam's loyalty, but the young man had his own plans.

Sahle Mariam's dream was to escape the fortress and become king of Shewa, as his father had been. Year after year passed, but he saw no chance to escape. By the year 1865, however, Tewodros was having so much trouble with England and with revolts inside his country that he eased up on guarding Sahle. Late one night in the summer of 1865, Sahle Mariam escaped with his mother and a few other prisoners. He immediately sent a short message to one of the emperor's enemies: "I have arrived. Send men to receive me."

Most of the people of Shewa welcomed the twenty-one-year-old Sahle Mariam as their king. The young king adopted the name Menilek II. The first Menilek had been the legendary son of King Solomon and the Queen of Sheba.

When Tewodros killed himself in 1868, twenty-four-year-old Menilek hoped to become emperor. But, after a struggle

with Menilek and several other leaders, Yohannes IV became emperor. For about twenty years Menilek built up his power and waited. He finally became emperor after Yohannes IV died of a battle wound in 1889.

Menilek was one of Ethiopia's best emperors. He introduced the country's first telephone, telegraph, railway, and banking systems. He and his wife, Empress Taitu, founded Addis Ababa, Ethiopia's capital. Menilek also worked to help farmers, and sometimes even worked out in the fields himself to show that "the farmer is closer to God than the king," as he once said.

Menilek's most famous moment came in the spring of 1896, when he and his forces defeated the Italians at the Battle of Adowa. Some historians say that this great Ethiopian victory paved the way for other African countries to rise up against their European rulers in the twentieth century. Menilek died at the age of sixty-nine after serving as emperor for twenty-four years.

HAILE SELLASSIE

Tafari Makonnen was born in 1892 near the town of Harar in Harerge Province. His father, Ras Makonnen was governor of the province and also cousin and close friend to Emperor Menilek II.

When Tafari was two years old, his mother died. Two years later, Tafari's father became a national hero by helping Menilek beat the Italians at the Battle of Adowa. Ras Tafari was expected to one day succeed Menilek as emperor, but in 1906 he died, leaving Tafari an orphan.

Fourteen-year-old Tafari Makonnen went to live at Menilek's palace in Addis Ababa, where he served as an assistant to the emperor. The intelligent young man was liked by Menilek and was expected to rise quickly to national prominence. However, between 1906 and 1908 Menilek suffered several paralyzing strokes. The reins of government were taken by Empress Taitu, who wanted her own relatives appointed to positions of power. Tafari wanted to be named governor of Harerge Province in his father's place, but, probably due to Taitu, in 1909 he was appointed governor of Sidamo Province, on the country's southern fringes.

The teenaged Tafari Makonnen, with little help, did a good job of governing Sidamo Province between 1909 and 1911. He assessed taxes, judged disputes, and fought the slave traders who entered the province. Meanwhile, back in Addis Ababa, Menilek's health was failing. Tafari had made some powerful friends in Addis Ababa, and when these men saw that the young man had done well as governor of Sidamo Province, they forced Taitu to appoint him governor of Harerge

Province. Glad to finally have his father's old position, Tafari Makonnen earned his people's respect for his fairness and modern ideas. Among other things, he lowered taxes for tenant farmers and banned forced labor.

In 1913 Menilek died and his grandson, Lij Iyasu, became emperor. After Lij Iyasu was deposed as emperor in 1916, Menilek's daughter, Zawditu, became empress and Tafari Makonnen was named regent to assist her.

One of Tafari's great achievements as regent was arranging for Ethiopia to be admitted to the League of Nations in 1923. A year later he became the first Ethiopian ruler to visit Europe when, accompanied by six lions and thirty assistants, he went to England, France, Belgium, Italy, and Greece.

By 1926 Tafari's power had far eclipsed Zawditu's. His army was so strong that in 1928 he forced the empress to make him a king, threatening to remove her from the throne if she refused. Then in 1930 Empress Zawditu died, and Tafari Makonnen became emperor that same year. He took as his throne name Haile Sellassie I, meaning "Power of the Trinity." During his first years as emperor, Haile Sellassie fought slavery, helped modernize Ethiopia's financial, public health, and education systems, and even donated large sums of his own money to build several schools.

Haile Sellassie led the effort to drive out the Italians after they invaded Ethiopia before World War II. While moving his army, he sometimes had to hide in caves to avoid Italian bombs. Some of his people were very angry when he left Ethiopia in the spring of 1936, because the emperor was supposed to die fighting rather than flee. But in 1941 he returned with English forces, which, with the help of Ethiopian troops, drove the Italians out of Ethiopia.

After World War II ended in 1945, Haile Sellassie gradually lost the respect of many Ethiopians, especially among college students and people who had traveled to other countries. Nation after nation in Africa adopted democratic forms of government, but Ethiopia remained a monarchy. Even when Haile Sellassie put forth a new constitution in 1955, he retained most of the power. There was a growing feeling that he cared more about keeping his power than about helping solve his country's massive problems.

By 1974 so many of his people opposed him that Haile Sellassie was helpless against a revolt by military forces. In September 1974, Haile Sellassie was imprisoned in his own palace as the dergue took power. Still a prisoner of the new government, Haile Sellassie died at age eighty-three in August 1975.

ABEBE BIKILA

Abebe Bikila was born about 1932 and grew up in a village about 100 miles (160 kilometers) north of Addis Ababa. Like most Ethiopians, Abebe was thin and short compared to people in Western countries. The skinny, barefoot young villager hardly seemed likely to become one of the greatest athletes of the century!

When Abebe was a young man, he was admitted to the Imperial Bodyguard. As part of their training, the men in the bodyguard attended a camp where they ran up to twenty miles (thirty-two kilometers) a day. All that running was difficult for most of the bodyguards, but twenty-four-year-old Abebe soon found that even twenty miles came fairly easy to him even though he had never run cross-country before. And he liked running so much that he was willing to work to become an even better runner.

In the summer of 1960, trials were held in Addis Ababa to select Ethiopia's team for the Olympic Games to be held that fall in Rome, Italy. Abebe Bikila did well in the marathon race trials, running the course in about two hours, forty minutes and then two hours, twenty-one minutes. Those times earned him a spot on the Olympic team, but no one gave Abebe much of a chance to win even the bronze medal in Rome.

On the September day that the Olympic marathon began in Rome, Abebe was the center of attention for a strange reason. He was running barefoot! The streets of Rome, some cobblestones, were like a bed of feathers compared to the rough Ethiopian terrain where Abebe also had run without shoes.

Early in the race Abebe was among the leaders, and by the halfway mark he was tied for first with a runner from Morocco. The two of them ran nearly side by side for over ten miles (sixteen kilometers). Then, with only a few miles left, the Moroccan made his move. Abebe gave it everything he had and surged into first place, pulling farther and farther ahead. By the end Abebe was an easy winner with a time of two hours, fifteen minutes, and sixteen seconds. Not only had the barefoot Ethiopian won the Olympic gold medal, but he had set a new world record for the marathon race!

In 1964 Abebe was again scheduled to go to the Olympic Games, this time in Tokyo, Japan. But several weeks before the Olympics, he had an emergency appendectomy. Abebe went with the team to Tokyo, but everyone thought he would do very poorly or miss the race entirely. Not only did Abebe run, but he again won the gold medal for the marathon. His time of two hours, twelve minutes, and eleven seconds was the new world record for the marathon (since broken) and he had become the first man to win the Olympic marathon race twice.

In 1968 Abebe tried to win his third straight Olympic gold medal, but a leg injury ruined his chances. However, Ethiopia claimed its third straight gold medal for the marathon when

The varied landscape near Yeha

Abebe's countryman, Mamo Wolde, won the race.

When not running, Abebe spent much of his time on Ethiopia's eastern border, where there was trouble with Somalia. But then, in 1969, Abebe's army and running careers both ended when he was permanently paralyzed in an automobile crash. The man who had once been the world's greatest marathon runner spent the rest of his life in a wheelchair. In 1973, almost exactly thirteen years after winning his first Olympic gold medal, Abebe Bikila died of a stroke at the age of forty-one.

MENGISTU HAILE MARIAM

Mengistu Haile Mariam was born in Addis Ababa in 1937. It is thought that his father may have been an Amhara nobleman and his mother a servant in the house. As a young man, he attended the Holeta Military School, which Haile Sellassie had established early in his reign as emperor.

For part of his military training, Mengistu was sent to the United States where he studied at the University of Maryland. It is thought that, while a student in the United States,

Mengistu developed his political philosophy. He became convinced that to correct the problems and injustices in their country, Ethiopians had to revolt against the emperor and set up a new government. He concluded that a Socialist form of government, similar to the Soviet Union, would be best for Ethiopia.

In 1960, Mengistu took part in the unsuccessful revolt against the emperor, Haile Sellassie spared the young man, and in 1974, Mengistu played a leading role in the successful revolution. He was one of the original members of the dergue, and in 1977 emerged as head of the Ethiopian government.

Mengistu was totally ruthless in his rise to power and in eliminating his enemies once he was in power. He was responsible for many thousands of killings, and has even been accused of letting hundreds of thousands of people die during the terrible famine of the mid-1980s.

Yet Mengistu also has done a great deal of good for his country. For example, he has helped the peasant farmers break away from the control of their former landlords, and he has made education available to many more Ethiopians than ever before.

MAP KEY

L. Abaya (lake)	4D	Dawa (river)	5E	Koram	4C		
L. Abe (lake)	5C	Debre Birhan	4D	Maji	4D		
Adami Tulu	4D	Debre Markos	4C	Massawa (Mesewa)	4B		
Addis Ababa	4D	Debre Tabor	4C	Mega	4E		
Adi Ugri	4C	Deder	5D	Mekdela	4C		
Adigrat	4C	Degeh Bur	5D	Mekele	4C		
Adwa (Adowa)	4C	Dekemhare	4B	Mendi	3D		
Agere Hiywet	4D	Dembidolo	3D	Mersa Fatma	5C		
Ahmar Mts.	5D	Dese	4C	Metema	4C		
Akesum (Aksum)	4C	Dila	4D	Mieso	5D		
Akobo (river)	3D	Dire Dawa	5D	Mojo	4D		
Akordat	4B	Dolo	5E	Moyale	4E		
Amhara Plateau	4D	Ed	5C	Nakfa	4B		
Ankober	4D	El Fud	5D	Nazaret	4D		
Arba Minch	4E	El Kere	5D	Negele	4D		
Arusi Province	4D	Eritrea Province	4B	Nekemte	4D		
Aseb	5C	Fafen (river)	5D	Om Hajer	4C		
Asela	4D	Fiche	4D	Ras Dashen (mountain)	4C		
Asmara (Asmera)	4B	Fik	5D	Sebderat	4B		
Asosa	3C	Gambela	3D	Sekota	4C		
Awasa	4D	Gemu Gofa Province	4D	Serdo	5C		
Awash	5D	Genale (river)	5D	L. Shala (lake)	4D		
Awash (river)	5C	Gidole	4D	Shashemene	4D		
Aysha	5C	Gilo (river)	3D	Shebele (river)	5D		
Bahir Dar (Bahar Dar)	4C	Ginir	5D	Shewa Gemira	4D		
Bako	4D	Goba	5D	Shewa Province	4D		
Bale Province	5D	Gojam Province	4C	Sidamo Province	4E		
Barentu	4B	Gondar (Gonder)	4C	Sodo	4D		
Baro (river)	3D	Gore	4D	L. Stefanie (lake)	4E		
Batu (mountain)	4D	Guna (mountain)	4C	Talo (mountain)	4C		
Begemdir and Simen (Gondar)		Hamoyet, Jabal (mountain)	4B	L. Tana (lake)	4C		
Province	4C	Harar (Harer)	5D	Tekeze River	4C		
Begi	3D	Harerge Province	5D	Tendaho	4C		
Beylul	5C	Ilubabor Province	3D	Teseney	5B		
Blue Nile (river)	4C, 4D	Imi	5D	Tigre (Tigray) Province	4C		
Bonga	4D	Jijiga	5D	Tiyo	5C		
Borama	5D	Jima	4D	Tulu Welel (mountain)	3D		
Choke Mountains	4C	Karkabet	4B	Waka	4D		
Dahlak Islands	5B	Kebri Dehar	5D	Welega Province	4D		
Danakil Plain		Kefa Province	4D	Welo Province	4C		
(Danakil Depression)	5C	Kelafo	5D	Wendo	4D		
Dangla	4C	Keren	4B	Yirqa Alem	4D		
		Korahe	5D	L. Zway (lake)	4D		

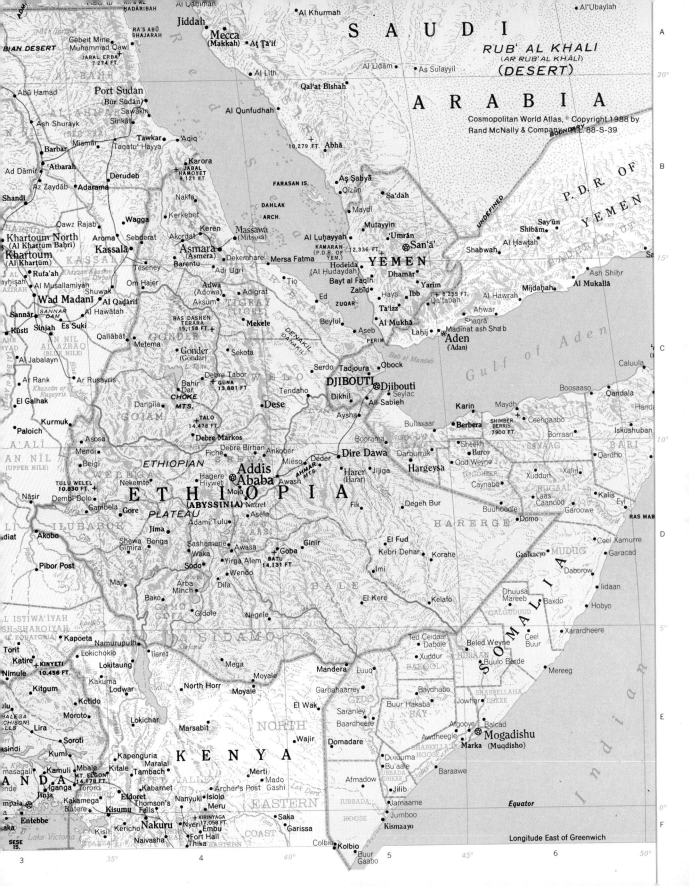

A religious festival in Addis Ababa

MINI-FACTS AT A GLANCE

GENERAL INFORMATION

Official Name: Hebretasebawi Etiyop'iya (Socialist Ethiopia)

Capital: Addis Ababa

Official Language: Amharic. English is the language of instruction in higher schools and is used along with Amharic in government documents. More than 95 languages and dialects are spoken.

Government: Virtually all powers of government are vested in the president by constitutional authority. The official ruling body is the National Shengo consisting of elected members of the Workers' Party of Ethiopia. Other important posts are held by military leaders.

Religion: Historically, the Ethiopian Orthodox church has had a strong influence comparable to that of the Catholic church on medieval Europe. But as a result of the revolution of 1974, it suffered many setbacks and lost its primacy as the official religion. The government recognized Islam as an official religion as well. About 40 percent of the people are Christians and about 40 percent are Muslims. There are a small number of Jews, who are known as Falashas, and some people still follow traditional African religions.

Flag: The national flag consists of three horizontal stripes—green, yellow, and red.

National Anthem: "Whedefit Gesgeshi Woude Henate Ethiopia" ("March Forward, Dear Mother Ethiopia, Bloom and Flourish")

Money: Basic unit—birr; in 1988, 2.07 Ethiopian birr equaled $1.00 in U.S. currency.

Weights and Measures: The metric system is used.

Population: Estimated 1988 population—42,403,000; 70 percent rural, 21 percent urban; 1984 census—42,019,418

113

Cities:

```
Addis Ababa . . . . . . . . . . . . . . . . . . . . . . . . . . . . . . . . . . . . . . . . . . . . . . 1,423,111
Asmara. . . . . . . . . . . . . . . . . . . . . . . . . . . . . . . . . . . . . . . . . . . . . . . . . .  373,800
Dire Dawa . . . . . . . . . . . . . . . . . . . . . . . . . . . . . . . . . . . . . . . . . . . . . . .  98,104
Harar . . . . . . . . . . . . . . . . . . . . . . . . . . . . . . . . . . . . . . . . . . . . . . . . . . .  70,289
Gondar. . . . . . . . . . . . . . . . . . . . . . . . . . . . . . . . . . . . . . . . . . . . . . . . . .  68,958
Dese . . . . . . . . . . . . . . . . . . . . . . . . . . . . . . . . . . . . . . . . . . . . . . . . . . . .  68,848
```
(Population figures based on 1984 census)

GEOGRAPHY

Highest Point: Ras Dashen, 15,158 ft. (4,620 m) above sea level

Lowest Point: Denakil Depression, 381 ft. (116 m) below sea level

Mountains: About two-thirds of the country is comprised of mountainous regions and plateaus. The western highlands lie at elevations between 8,000 to 12,000 ft. (2,498 and 3,657 m). The northern end of this region is in northern Eritrea, where erosion has cut down to base rock. In the Simen Mountains is the highest peak. The tablelands are crosscut by deep gorges and canyons and surrounded by grassy and desert lands.

The eastern highlands have a largely basaltic cover, and the highest area is a mountain chain that runs along the valley, sloping steeply on its eastern side.

Rivers: The major rivers are the Blue Nile, the Tekeze, and the Baro. In the inland drainage area are the Awash River, which flows northward, and the Omo River, which flows southward. In the area of southeasternly drainage are the Webi, Genale, and the Dawa rivers, which join to form the Juba and the Shebele.

Climate: Although Ethiopia is completely within tropical latitudes, it enjoys a temperate climate in the Highland areas. The range of temperature is small because Ethiopia is so close to the equator. On the Amhara Plateau minimum temperatures are felt during the cloudy and rainy months (mid-June through mid-September), whereas maximum temperatures are the rule during clear, sunny periods. Temperatures range from 60° F. (15° C) during the wet season to 70° degrees F. (20° C) during the dry season.

Lower altitudes bring higher readings, with 80° F. (25° C) being common during the wet season and 95° F. (35° C) during the dry.

The total annual rainfall is 20 to 30 in. (50 to 75 cm).

Greatest Distances: North to south—1,020 mi. (1,642 km)
East to west—1,035 mi. (1,666 km)

Area: 471,800 sq. mi. (1,221,900 km²)

NATURE

Trees: Forests occupy about 4 percent of the total area of the country. The southwestern rain forests, found mainly in Kefa and Ilubabor, are composed of large broad-leaved trees and a thick undergrowth of ferns, creepers, and bushes, including the coffee bush. At higher altitudes the subtropical forests are dominated by the yellowwood, an evergreen tree with a pulpy fruit. Still higher are the coniferous forests, dominated by the juniper. In the lowlands the most widespread tree is the acacia. The eucalyptus is common in inhabited regions.

Animals: The walia ibex (a type of mountain goat) is found in the mountains, as are the mountain nyala, the Abyssinian jackal, and the gelada baboon. Various kinds of wild pig occur in large numbers. Many smaller animals, from the aardvark to the white-tailed mongoose, are widespread in southern areas.
The largest wildlife areas are the lower Omo valley, the Awash valley, the Gambela region of Ilubabor, and the southwest. Animals include lions, elephants, leopards (now quite rare), buffalo, zebras, giraffes, and black rhinoceroses (also quite rare). Crocodiles, hippopotamuses, rhinoceroses, and pythons live close to the rivers.

Birds: Among the world's widest variety of birds live in Ethiopia. They include ostriches, pelicans, flamingos, storks, egrets, ibises, larks, eagles, hawks, shrikes, vultures, hornbills, and bee-eaters.

Fish: Commercial fishing is restricted to the Red Sea coastal waters. But techniques are poor and the role of fishing in the traditional economy is limited due to poor techniques and equipment and dependence on foreign markets.

EVERYDAY LIFE

Food: One of the most popular foods is a thick and spicy stew called *wat*. It is made from meat or pulses (lentils, peas, and beans) and sometimes eggs are added to it. A slightly sour pancake-shaped bread called *injera* is a staple of the Ethiopian diet. *Teff* is the choice cereal grain for making bread, though barley, sorghum, corn, and wheat are also of major importance.

Beans, lentils, and peas are favorite sources of protein. Onions, garlic, Irish potatoes, greens, and pumpkins are the only vegetables consumed regularly in cooked form. Many wild fruits—such as lemons—and commercially grown oranges and grapefruit are available but are rarely eaten.

A favorite alcoholic drink is *talla*, a beer fermented from barley and the leaves of the *gesho* plant. *Tej*, which is more alcoholic than talla, is more costly and therefore consumed only by wealthier inhabitants.

Famine has been extensive and devastating during several seasons during the last few decades.

Housing: The most common type of house, which predominates in the villages, in rural sections of the highlands, and to some degree in the outskirts of cities, is the circular, conical—roofed *gocho*. The walls are made of strong, upright poles set close together in the ground. Other poles are set horizontally to form a latticed frame. In grain-growing areas stalks are tied to the poles and mud packing make the walls. In bamboo areas bamboo is the cover. The floors are earthen. There is usually one entrance and no windows. In urban areas a number of rectangular houses also are found, with roofs of thatch materials or corrugated iron sheeting.

From 50 to 79 percent of urban inhabitants live in one-room houses. Approximately 60 percent have no indoor plumbing, and only a small percentage are equipped for electricity.

Holidays:

> January 7, Christmas Day
> January 19, Feast of the Epiphany
> February 19, Martyrs' Day
> March 2, Commemoration of the Battle of Adowa
> March or April, Good Friday; Easter Sunday
> May 5, Liberation Day
> August 22, Feast of the Assumption
> September 11, New Year's Day
> September 12, Ethiopia National Day
> September 27, Feast of the Finding of the True Cross

Culture: Christianity has been the predominant cultural influence in Ethiopia. The national literature, both past and present, is Christian in orientation. Chronicles describing the kings began to be produced on parchment in the late thirteenth century.

Oral tradition is strong in the south, west, and southeast. Somalis are known for memorizing and retaining their oral poetry.

A unique literary form is "wax and gold" poetry, developed by the Amhara hundreds of years ago, and written on many subjects—politics, religion, and romance. A number of Amharic plays have been written, mainly since the liberation, and are performed either at the national theater or under the auspices of the university.

Christian traditional art was largely Byzantine in style. Painting centers on the church, and modern artists, too, often choose religious subjects.

Many songs and dances performed in the Ethiopian church date from the 500s, and musicians have long roamed the countryside. There also are a small but flourishing school of music and a school of fine art, founded in 1966, both run by Ethiopians trained in the United States.

Sports and Recreation: Soccer is gaining acceptance as the national sport. Major sports competition exists in volleyball, tennis, track and field, boxing, and swimming. Card games, chess, and other board games are popular pastimes. Ethiopian athletes won gold medals in the marathon and made notable showings in track and field in the Olympics of 1960, 1964, and 1968.

Addis Ababa offers the variety of recreational activities found in many large Western cities.

Communication: All facilities are government owned and operated. Telephone lines first laid by Menilek II were greatly extended during the Italian occupation. Service with the outside world also has been extended. A World Bank loan in 1951 made possible the installation of an automatic telephone exchange in the capital and access to worldwide circuits.

About half a dozen daily newspapers are published. At least eleven weekly papers and approximately thirty periodicals appear at less frequent intervals. The press seldom informs the public about political activities. Short, factual accounts of government affairs appear occasionally in the Addis Ababa press, but the details of the issues involved must depend on word-of-mouth dissemination.

Transportation: At the beginning of the twentieth century, modern transportation of any kind was virtually absent, but by now the country has some roads, a railway line, and an airline with well-developed domestic and international services. The major roads radiate from Addis Ababa. Most of them do not extend to the borders.

Water transport is undeveloped. Most rivers are not navigable, and of the lakes, only Tana has transport of any economic significance.

Schools: Traditional education is almost solely the concern of religious institutions. The modern school system introduced by Emperor Menilek II was greatly expanded and developed. It is still inadequate, however; 70 percent of the population is illiterate.

The main institution of higher learning is Addis Ababa University. Asmara University was founded after the 1974 revolution.

Health and Welfare: The bulk of the population must rely on traditional methods of medical treatment, such as herbal medicines and holy waters. Modern medical care reaches only a fraction of the people.

Communicable diseases such as malaria and tuberculosis are prevalent. Leprosy is fought with international help. All bodies of water except Lake Langano are infested with a schistosomes, which cause disease. Preventive medicine is hampered by a shortage of facilities and trained personnel, poor drinking water, and poor nutrition.

Principal Products:

Agriculture: coffee, corn, cotton, sugar cane, oilseeds, sorghum, teff, wheat, barley
Manufacturing: cigarettes, cement, refined petroleum products, shoes, textiles, processed foods

IMPORTANT DATES:

2000 B.C. — An Egyptian names Hennu sails to the Land of Punt — possibly Ethiopia

1000 B.C. — People from Arabia sail across the Red Sea and enter what is now northern Ethiopia

400s B.C. — Two major groups inhabit the area — the Cushites and the Semites

A.D. 200s — Aksum kingdom established in what is now Ethiopia

326 — Ezana becomes king. Christianity becomes the official religion after he is baptized in 340

Early seventh century — Islam founded in Saudi Arabia by the prophet Muhammad

1137 — Zagwe Dynasty rises to power

1270 — Yekuno Amalak overthrows Zagwe Dynasty

1769-1855 — Ethiopian Empire breaks up into small kingdoms

1855-68—Tewodros II is emperor; Ethiopia begins to emerge from medieval isolation

1869—Suez Canal opens

1889—Menilek II becomes emperor

1896—Battle of Adowa; Menilek defeats Italian army

1913—Menilek dies; Lij Iyasu becomes emperor

1916—Lij Iyasu removed from power with help of Great Britain, France, and Italy. Ras Tafari Makonnen named regent and successor to throne

1923—Ethiopia admitted to League of Nations

1930—Haile Sellassie I (Ras Tafari Makonnen) crowned as emperor

1931—First written constitution

1935—Italy invades Ethiopia

1936—Italians conquer Addis Ababa; Haile Sellassie flees to Great Britain

1941—World War II: British troops help Ethiopians drive Italians out of the country; Haile Sellassie returns to the throne

1945—United Nations is born; Ethiopia is one of the original members

1952—In UN plebicite, Eritrea votes to join Ethiopia

1960—Haile Sellassie quells a revolt

1962—Haile Sellassie abrogates Eritrea's federated status

1972-74—Severe drought leads to famine in the northeast

1974—Haile Sellassie removed from power; Provisional Military Administrative Council (PMAC) seizes control

1976—Military assistance agreement with Soviet Union

1977 — Ethiopia closes United States military missions

1977-78 — Red Terror; campaign against opposition by PMAC

1984-85 — Several hundred thousand Ethiopians die of hunger and its accompanying diseases

1987 — Ethiopia adopts new constitution that provides for return to civilian government; yet military leaders continue to hold power; famine grips Ethiopia again

1988 — Famine continues

IMPORTANT PEOPLE:

Abebe Bikela (1932-73), runner; Olympic gold medalist, 1960, 1964

Afewerk Tekle, artist, executed stained-glass windows in Africa Hall in Addis Ababa

Ahmed ibn Ibrahim al-Ghazi (Ahmed Gran) (1506-43), Muslim leader who attacked Ethiopia in 1527

Girmane Neway (d. 1961), staged revolt against Haile Sellassie in 1960

Haile Sellassie I (Ras Tafari Makonnen), (1892-1975), became emperor in 1930; deposed in 1974

Lij Iyasu (1896-1935), nephew of Menilek II, emperor 1911-16

Mamo Wolde, Olympic runner; gold medalist, 1968

Mengistu Haile Mariam (1937-   ), political leader; set up Socialist government 1974

Mengistu Neway (d. 1961), led revolt against Haile Sellassie in 1960

Menilek II (1844-1913), succeeded to throne in 1899

Miruts Yifter, Olympic gold medalist, 5,000 and 10,000 meters, 1980

Ras Tafari Makonnen, *see Haile Sellassie I*

Tewodros II (1818-68), emperor from 1855 to 1868

Yohannes IV (1831-89), emperor from 1872 to 1889

INDEX

Page numbers that appear in boldface type indicate illustrations

About the Author

Dennis Fradin is the author of nearly 100 children's books. His previous books for Childrens Press include ASTRONOMY and the DISASTER! series. His recent works include REMARKABLE CHILDREN, a nonfiction book published by Little, Brown; HOW I SAVED THE WORLD, a science-fiction novel published by Dillon Press; and a series of biographies on CO-LONIAL AMERICANS for Enslow Publishers. He has also written stories and articles for many magazines including *The Saturday Evening Post*, *Scholastic*, *National Humane Review*, and *Illinois Issues*.

Dennis is married to a high-school teacher named Judy. They have a daughter, Diana, and two sons, Tony and Michael. In his free time, Dennis enjoys stargazing with his telescope and playing baseball.

40129